Medical Staff Integration

Transactions and Transformation

Larry Boress, President and CEO, Midwest Business Group on Health

"Mike La Penna brings an important perspective to a key shift in the structure of health care. Providers, payers, employers, and patients are greatly impacted by this shift from relative independence to integration, which has critical implications to the cost and quality of health care as we know it today."

Robert Harrison, MHA, PhD., President, Lake Michigan College; Former President of the Michigan Hospital Association and hospital board member

"There is no more complex administrative environment than health care and no time when it has been more confusing and challenging. Mr. La Penna has outlined several of the models and structures that go well beyond the traditional medical staff relationships. His book is recommended reading for the practitioner, the administrator, and the board level stakeholders as they contemplate how to work together in the new health care environment."

George O. Waring III, MD, FACS, FRCOphth, Professor of Ophthalmology, Emeritus, Emory University; private clinical practice, Atlanta, GA

"After 25 years of my seeking Michael La Penna's counsel and direction in half a dozen different medical practice venues and models, I have learned to appreciate his incisiveness, his conciseness, his analytical skills, his wisdom, and his dry humor. A survey of the 21 chapter titles gives a good clue to the superb information in this contemporary and masterful book."

Susan Mendelowitz, RN FACHE, President and COO, Bergen Regional Medical Center, Paramus, NJ

Paul C. Mendelowitz, MD, MPH, Former Chief Medical Officer, Holy Name Medical Center, Teaneck, NJ

"Mike La Penna is the consummate medical staff business consultant. His impressive depth of knowledge coupled with his common sense approach has led to successful resolution of a broad array of issues we have faced in managing the business organization, compensation, and management of our physicians and their practices. His words of wisdom and advice regarding physician integration are welcome in this turbulent time of reform and aggregation of health care entities."

Dr. Anthony J. Gagliardi, MD, Vice President & Chief Medical Officer, New York Presbyterian Lower Manhattan Hospital and Charter Trustee of SERVITAS IPA of Greater New York

"No health care environment is tougher than New York. When change occurs, it is rapid and dramatic. We look to experts who have a proven track record of managing change. Mike La Penna assisted us with the development of an IPA that numbered over 5,000 providers and a dozen institutions at a time when managed care first emerged. He fashioned the governance as well as the value proposition for all of the stakeholders. I welcome any book that captures his expertise and experience."

Ahmed Abdelsalam, MD, FACS, Managing Partner of Chicagoland Retinal Consultants, LLC.

"In this time of turmoil and turbulence in relations between hospitals and their medical staff members, and with all the different models emerging, it is a help to have a concise review of the options along with practical examples of structure, governance, and income distribution. This book is a primer on how hospitals and doctors can find common ground to move from independence to collaboration to some level of true integration."

William Cunningham, DO, MHA, Assistant Dean College of Osteopathic Medicine, Michigan State University

"In the process of working in clinical and administrative medical positions for decades, I have had the pleasure of doing a number of joint projects with Mr. La Penna and his team. I am enthused to see that the experience and insight of his years of consulting in the hospital-physician ecosystem have finally made it into print. Anyone who is working with physician transactions will find some solace in knowing that some of us have been there before! This book suggests a number of ways to improve the reader's chances of succeeding in the very complex world of the new medical staff."

Medical Staff Integration

Transactions and Transformation

A. Michael La Penna

CRC Press is an imprint of the
Taylor & Francis Group, an **informa** business
A PRODUCTIVITY PRESS BOOK

CRC Press
Taylor & Francis Group
6000 Broken Sound Parkway NW, Suite 300
Boca Raton, FL 33487-2742

First issued in hardback 2019

ISBN-13: 978-1-4665-9296-4 (hbk)

Library of Congress Cataloging-in-Publication Data

La Penna, A. Michael, author.
Medical staff integration : transactions and transformation / A. Michael La Penna.
p. ; cm.
Includes bibliographical references and index.
ISBN 978-1-4665-9296-4 (hardcover : alk. paper)
I. Title.
[DNLM: 1. Hospital Administration--United States. 2. Medical Staff, Hospital--United States. 3. Models, Organizational--United States. 4. Partnership Practice--United States. 5. Physicians--United States. 6. Practice Management, Medical--United States. WX 150 AA1]

RA972
362.11068--dc23 2014017608

Visit the Taylor & Francis Web site at
http://www.taylorandfrancis.com

and the CRC Press Web site at
http://www.crcpress.com

This book is dedicated to my two younger physician-brothers, Bob and Bill. Both are healers and clinicians, first and foremost, and each embodies the "old school" approach to medicine: "If you take care of the patient, everything else will take care of itself." Both are graduates of the Michigan State School of Human Medicine, and both followed a path to interventional cardiology by way of Henry Ford. Each will be remembered by their patients as caring and compassionate physicians who spent their lives in the clinic, on call, and in consultation with other doctors, and, most importantly, with their patients and their families.

No sense going through any kind of clinical or medical background on them except to remark that they are both rather naïve about the business side of the health care delivery system, and neither knows much about what this book is about, or cares. Bob is a master diagnostician when it comes to all things automotive, and Bill is the collector and curator of what is probably the most extensive collection of brewerania* in the United States. Both focus on being good fathers and great siblings. Neither of them cares whether he is "in" or "out" of whatever local "integrated" health care network is currently emerging (or diverging or destructing), but each is actively practicing as if the patient he is with is the only part of "population health" that matters.

* Brewerania is the term for advertising paraphernalia related to brewing, breweries, and beer.

Contents

Author's note: Models and monographs and charts contained in this book can be downloaded at the companion web site MEDICALSTAFFINTEGRATION.com

Acknowledgments

I especially thank all of those who contributed to this book by sharing with me their knowledge and background of ambulatory care processes, medical systems delivery, and benefit design, and how all of these factors of delivery work together, and especially what happens when they do not. I am indebted to Jeff Beird, who originated many of the concepts and models related to valuation, on which some of the technical material in this book is based. In addition, most of the concepts in this book are borrowed and, in some cases, lifted directly from material developed by Dorothea Taylor, who has spent decades in the front lines of physician practice management. Her insight is derived from direct problem solving and from the on-site application of sound business practices and organization theory to the consumer and the provider engagement process. Any operational wisdom or practical observations that are offered in this book have been borrowed from work she proofed in the field. Where possible, I have credited Jeff and Dorothea, but the reader should note that the entire book is based on their insight and the many projects that we have managed over decades of consulting. I am also indebted to the many clients of our firm, hospitals, and doctors, who for three decades have allowed us to assist them in a variety of transactional and transitional challenges. We have learned much more from our clients than they ever learned from us.

A. Michael La Penna

Introduction—New Models Using Refashioned Parts

There are a few select authors and futurists who most of us reference when planning and prognosticating about health care and its future forms. If any definitive list existed, it would most certainly contain futurists and academicians like Jeff Goldsmith, Leland Kaiser, Uwe Reinhard, and Edward F.X. Hughes.* Each has addressed the topic of health care transition and the future of health care by focusing on his own special area of study and expertise. However, when one looks over their collected writings, blogs, and presentations, we find that they were among the first to recognize health care as a system of providers and institutions, payers and patients, who are interconnected and interrelated in an economic and functional form. They each have recognized that what we casually refer to as "integration" can be measured and studied, and that it has a unique value. I am not sure who advanced this idea first, but I suspect that these and other great minds always conceived of the health care delivery system differently than the practitioners and providers within it and the markets that have actually shaped it.

Hospitals and physicians exist in the same marketplace providing complementary services to the same consumer population under the same payment mechanisms. They do so in a combination of transactions that are defined along traditional lines, but which are generally referred to as *fee for service*. However, this concept has often blurred over the past decades, especially since the advent of payment structures that have been designed by intermediate payers like Medicare and the managed care organizations that organize payments from self-funded employers

* Health care futurist references can be further studied at their individual web source pages: Leland R. Kaiser, PhD, http://www.kaiser.net/lee-kaiser; Jeff Goldsmith, PhD, http://www.healthfutures.net/index.php; Edward F.X. Hughes, MD, MPH, http://www.kellogg.northwestern.edu/Faculty/Directory/Hughes_Edward.aspx#biography; Uwe E. Reinhard, PhD, http://wws.princeton.edu/people/display_person.xml?netid=reinhard&display=C.

and standard insured products. There are some generalities that can be made about how doctors and hospitals interrelate and overlap, but the most basic observation is that physicians join a voluntary medical staff at a hospital and direct their patients to that institution for a variety of inpatient and outpatient care. However, this generalization is never the only relationship that exists between doctors in any specific hospital. The more precise generalization is that doctors and hospitals have a variety of collaborative and competitive processes and arrangements that make up a collection of relationships that merge in a series of events that cause care to be provided directly to patients; but the payment comes indirectly from government programs and other private intermediaries.

Generally speaking, no generalizations can be easily made. The many alternate systems that are emerging are doing so in similar formats but at differing speeds and through different channels. There are basic trends that are pretty well accepted by anyone who is watching the structure of the health care system. One trend that is unmistakable is that more doctors are moving from private and independent practice to more formal business models that include the hospital as a direct partner of some kind. Often, these models include a transaction that is something like a purchase and a result that is something like employment for the doctors. The trend is straightforward, but while it is simple to describe, it reflects a series of complex transactions that occur in even a more complex regulatory environment. The health care system is headed toward practices and physicians being operated by health care systems that are, in turn, operating to serve consumer health mechanisms that are driven by new forms of information exchanges and payment structures. These operational delivery units are in transition at the same time that the payment structures that are being designed to fund them are in their own formative stages.

The entire health care system, providers and payers, is also being shaped by the unknown factor of additional demand from the many Americans who will soon be insured in some form under the Patient Protection and Affordable Care Act (PPACA).* By the end of 2014, physicians and hospitals will be serving an additional 40 million patients in a new form of payment system that references value in some form of a quality and price measurement matrix that has yet to be fully developed and defined.

Health care systems will have been formed from competing entities that have developed their relationships based upon undefined but anticipated health care payment structures and unproven and unpredictable reimbursement formulae. Consumers will be choosing their entry into this new marketplace with tools that are still under development. We know that the consumer is presently choosing his

* Enacted in 2010, the Patient Protection and Affordable Care Act has a timeline that is being implemented over a 4-year period that includes new forms of health care delivery (accountable care organizations) and new methodologies for health care payment (insurance exchanges). A complete timeline can be found on the government's consumer-oriented website http://www.healthcare.gov/law/timeline/full.html#2014.

or her care with some kind of information that is generally derived from a trusted health care advisor of some kind, or simply by chance, which can be influenced by advertising and geographic location. Soon, they will have new information channels, most of which will be operating on as yet unformed assumptions and on questionable data. Consumer choice will meet the health care system at a junction where the demand function is based on sparse information and where the supply process is still under construction.

Health care is a marketplace that has not yet benefited from the information technology boom, which is reshaping choice in general consumer services and wholesale pricing. As a consumer with a tablet or a cell phone, I can compare refrigerators and appliances on every level by which they can be measured and source reviews from credible consumer agencies and from other consumers like myself. I can also order a pizza online and watch a timeline for its development and delivery. However, I cannot make an appointment for health care services or get the results from yesterday's blood tests.* More importantly, I can gauge price from a number of different suppliers and choose services that can be compared side by side. Any consumer that has compared credit card deals or airfare pricing or cell phone plans will understand the problem with pricing transparency in health care. The problem, simply stated, is that there is none.

The lack of comparative quality and price data is partially true because of a variety of information debates that are confusing patient privacy with the patient's need for information access, but largely it is due to the fact that the health care industry is sadly underpowered when it comes to the capitalization of information technology and the packaging of information in any usable format for the patients or for the providers† that serve them.

At the present moment, over 50% of the population is covered by some form of a managed care organization (MCO). There are almost 70 million Americans in HMOs and over 100 million enrolled in preferred provider organizations (PPOs). Another 35 million are in "point of service" plans and consumer high-deductible

* Some readers will be quick to point out that they can get some appointments online and that there are doctors who will respond by e-mail. These are fulfillment services that are not yet truly integrated. Domino's Pizza® has a more integrated appointment function than the largest of the health care systems operating in 2013–2014, and places that warehouse appliances offer more complete information on their products than the most advanced integrated health system.

† Throughout this book, the term *providers* is used to reflect any professional who dispenses medical care directly. Physicians would be a more common term, but that does not recognize that there are physician assistants and nurse practitioners who also have varying degrees of practice autonomy and who will comprise a significant portion of the space devoted to health care access in the future. These provider categories are under constant transformation in every state, and the only generalization that can be made is that their roles are being expanded on every level and their involvement will be generally accepted in many areas that were formerly the domain of the physician.

payment programs.* This trend is soon to be expanded dramatically by the growth that will occur as Medicare and other social programs continue to toy with managed care initiatives. The Affordable Care Act (ACA) implementation will also fuel the continued development of managed care. Generally, and arguably, this trend has produced cost savings for the payers of care, be they employers or public agencies. One can argue that the quality of care has not been in any way hampered by these payment mechanisms, and some would advance the notion that the care has actually improved. Physicians generalize that managed care makes their practice more difficult and the business of running a practice infinitely more challenging.† Simply put, the challenge for a physician practice to somehow thrive from a different, more complex, payment system is daunting. The typical physician practice simply does not have the critical mass of patients or the infrastructure to capitalize on the many changes that have been introduced in the health care system over the past couple of decades. This is only going to get worse, and the doctors know it.

This book is not about why this is all occurring, nor is it intended to cover the areas that question how the health care system should be changed. This book is all about what is happening and how physicians and hospitals should think about the changes that are trending now and which will be erupting at different stages all across the country. This is a book that attempts to address these changes in a nonjudgmental fashion and from a business case perspective. Hopefully, it will allow a reader to gain an understanding of some of the basics behind the various types of relationships that are forming and assist in the nuts and bolts of the transactions and the transitions that will result. As for transformation of the health care system, there is no one who really understands what will emerge after the changes underway are complete. Maybe, if the appropriate incentives are aligned in some way—consumer, society, institution, and physician—the result will be a more stable and effective health care system and one that matches access and technology and care and prevention to bring the promise of these factors to bear on areas of greatest need and at a price that we all can afford. Few of the futurists that I referenced in the opening paragraphs of this Introduction are confident that this will actually occur.

---

* The Managed Care Fact Sheet from MCOL (http://www.mcol.com/current_enrollment), reporting statistics from 2010, 2011, and 2012 derived from Kaiser State Health Facts; Healthleaders, Inc., Special Data Request, May 2011; Kaiser/HRET Employer Health Benefit Survey—September 2011; U.S. Census Bureau, Income, Poverty and Health Insurance Coverage in the United States: 2010; AAPPO Press Release, April 25, 2011. Data source: Mercer National Survey of Employer Sponsored Health Plans.

† In numerous physician consultations over the past 30 years, we have been asked often by doctors how to make money in managed care. Our stock answer has been, "Buy HMO company stock." This is not really a flip comment since HMOs have done pretty well over that period of time, and most doctors will complain that the fee-for-service business model cannot thrive in a managed care-controlled environment.

About the Author

Mike La Penna has been a consultant to physician groups and hospitals for more than 25 years. He has served in a number of board positions on health care organizations and community service organizations. He has been an executive in both nonprofit and for-profit health care environments.

Mike is a graduate of the University of Chicago's Graduate School of Business, where he earned an MBA and a certificate in health care administration. He has a BA in economics from Western Michigan University, and he has held faculty positions in both undergraduate and graduate business programs.

Mike's expertise includes strategic planning, payer negotiation, real estate ventures, merger, acquisition, and divestiture strategies, product branding, independent provider association (IPA)/physician-hospital organization (PHO) development and management, equity and risk arrangements, technology applications, and faculty group practice plans. The La Penna Group, Inc. was founded in 1987 to provide business consulting services to physicians, hospitals, and health care delivery systems. It has also worked with industry and with governmental units to develop solutions for a variety of health care delivery situations. He has been an advisor to numerous national associations and authored numerous articles on health care trends, physician practice management, and network development. He has commented on health care for numerous publications and news outlets, including Crain's, the *Wall Street Journal*, the *New York Times*, and NPR. Mr. La Penna is an advisor to some of the world's largest health care delivery organizations and to numerous Fortune 100 firms.

Chapter 1

Conceptualizing New Models of Care Based on Traditional Structures

Originally, the cost savings that were perceived to be delivered by many managed care organization (MCO) programs were associated with the more centralized model types, such as group-oriented and staff model health maintenance organizations (HMOs). Hospitals attempted to emulate these forms using a variety of organizational structures, and in most cases, these proved to be inefficient and unmanageable and unable to assume and control the risk associated with capitated contracts. Figure 1.1 demonstrates the basic variety of medical staff and physician relationships with hospitals in a form that shows that there are only a couple of cost avoidance and cost control mechanisms that have been tried over the years. These are arrayed in a fashion that uses a Boston Consulting grid* to organize the idea of cost control with certainty.

Lower on the vertical axis represents more costly programming, and the left side of the matrix reflects less certainty. So, if one were to choose in a rational sense, the bias would be toward less costly programs with more certainty of some kind of performance. Arguably, the categories may be incomplete and the assignment of weights may be wrong, but the concept is simple to use in discussing how the process facing health care purchasers has evolved from one of buying programs and

* *Boston Consulting grid* and *Boston Consulting matrix* are terms that are used to describe a two-by-two graphic representation that is used as a planning tool to assist in ranking any number of ideas. It was originally introduced as a concept in the 1970s by the Boston Consulting Group.

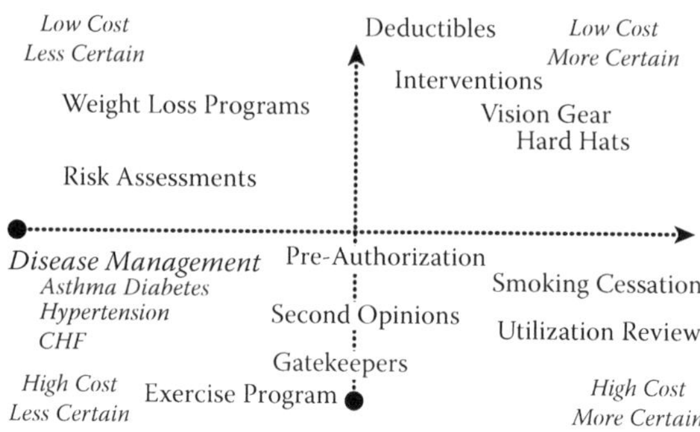

Figure 1.1 The only real information contained above that is relatively assured is that interventions like flu shots and safety equipment are pretty effective and cheap. They are properly placed in the matrix. Higher cost areas of endeavor with no real research supporting their value proposition are probably also pretty clearly defined. Most of the programs are open to the reader's speculation as to their value.

program components to simply accepting the fact that there may not be enough credible information to even use in arguing about the placement of programming on a two-by-two matrix. The purchasers simply do not have the tools to understand how these factors might be judged.

Increasingly, however, both research and the health care cost experience of large corporations have shown that the newer MCO models working with their own networks of providers, such as independent provider associations (IPAs) and preferred provider organizations (PPOs), can also achieve changes in the health care cost structure, particularly when affiliated with networks of care developed by self-funded employers or large insurance companies. The savings do not reverse the *trend* of cost for health care (it is still on the rise), but they can control the rates of increase in costs. Predesigned networks average about one-half of the increase experienced in traditional fee-for-service markets. Thus, the answer for the purchaser may not be a program but a mechanism for contracting that provides results.

Hospitals, sensing this trend, realize that their need is to be within a network instead of outside it. As with any institution, the preference is to have some kind of control. This is natural since the hospital may represent a major component of the cost of the health care that is to be contracted through the network, and it may have the most capital invested in the network structure. Also, the hospital generally already has an infrastructure of some kind that can be deployed to support network initiatives. Where IPAs include a hospital, the acronym that results is generally PHO—physician-hospital organization. Instead of defining the market and providing an innovative product form, these provider-focused organizations have been a response to changes that either are occurring or are thought to soon occur. This structure emulates a traditional medical staff, and it attempts to reformat it into a more effective contracting entity.

Consolidation is underway in a variety of forms. There are no factors that will reverse the trends of increasing costs and advancing consolidation in health care both on the payer side and in the provider community. Government programs such as the PPACA have recognized this fact and have been structured around the existing and emerging infrastructures. However, past attempts under the Clinton administration failed, and any form that tries to build a new solution upon a structure that is made from the existing payment strategies is probably going to be lacking. The PPACA is often called an insurance reform act rather than a health care bill because it really only repackages insurance programs in a different format, leaving the traditional infrastructure in place. The reform process is really just an attempt to guide the present programs in a more rational and functional manner. There is not any real guarantee that it will be effective, but the supply side of the market is already reorganizing to respond.

PPACA changes are made more confusing for providers because they are driven by a national process, but they can also be specific to each state. There is a continuing shift to managed care, the impact of which on providers will go from substantial to more substantial, but it will differ depending upon how the states enroll in various parts of the programming. States, being unique in their social programming and generally distinctive, will enact different approaches under the PPACA umbrella of regulation and against a backdrop of multistate insurance exchanges. The impact of this shift on managed care companies will also be monumental, but they are structured to be able to respond to changes in funds management, broad pricing strategies, and shifts in market factors. The networks are generally not structured to take on the changes that are occurring or which are about to occur.

The following summary is an opinionated definition of the strengths and weaknesses of each type of network that has arisen over the past couple of decades.

Physician-Hospital Organization (PHO)

A PHO is a legal entity formed by a hospital and a group of physicians to further mutual interests and achieve market objectives. A PHO generally combines physicians and hospital into a single organization for the purpose of obtaining payer contracts. Doctors maintain their ownership of individual practices. They agree to accept managed care patients according to the terms of a professional services agreement with the PHO. The PHO serves as a collective negotiating and contracting unit. In many cases, a PHO operates with other corporate structures under its control (like an IPA or a management services organization (MSO)). A PHO is generally managed by a board that is a combined hospital and physician committee.

Its challenges include membership, governance structure, financial viability, and control over its members. Generally, a PHO has difficulty dealing with sophisticated pricing and performance strategies. For the purposes of definition, a PHO that is not a single source for contracting (that cannot contract on behalf of its members) is little more than a social arrangement. If a PHO is to be effective, it must be able to contract as a single business unit.

Independent Provider Association (IPA)

An IPA is a legal entity chartered under state law to contract on behalf of physician groups (and other providers) who are otherwise operating independently. It is generally formed in an environment where the doctors need to collaborate on risk sharing or gain sharing or some other form of collective contracting effort. The physician practices are not merged, and the IPA is not empowered to develop joint ventures, provide services, or otherwise act for purposes outside its charter. The IPA can have several contracts if allowed to do so by the state in which it is chartered, and it can organize capital for risk pool offsets and for funding reserves.

The challenge of an IPA is that none of its members perceive it as anything but a contracting vehicle. It charges dues, but it does not generally have a sophisticated infrastructure that is built on a basis of an information exchange or a common medical information platform. Its limitation is identified by its very name—*independent* provider association. This is a club that consists of practices and physicians who do not want to be in a club. They hope that they can forestall the advent of system change by selectively contracting in a form that emulates the traditional business model of the private fee-for-service medical practice. This is basically a transitional form that exists in select markets only when recognized by payers. When they no longer need this format, it will become extinct or irrelevant, as it has already in many markets.

Contracting Unit/Messenger Model

In this type of organization, the doctors contract with an independent "messenger" who works with the managed care organizations to outline pricing and contract provisions. The doctors never discuss prices or collaborate on contract components as a group. Some IPAs operate in this fashion. The messenger negotiates opportunities for the group, but each individual practitioner is allowed to determine, individually and independently, if there is interest for participation.

This model was one that was used to augment or replace IPAs where groups of doctors were challenged by either state sanctions or their own fierce independence to maintain final control over their fee structures and contract participation. It is worthy to note, only to reference that it was never an efficient model, and any model that was not efficient in the past will not be part of the future of health care contracting.

Management Services Organization (MSO)

An MSO is a legal entity that provides administrative and practice management services to physicians. A physician practice then contracts with the MSO for services. An MSO does not enter into risk arrangements, and it is not designed to manage risk pools or withholds (or develop reserves). The MSO, like any management service, can assist the doctors in determining their response to managed care and pricing issues. The role of the MSO can vary, as can its ownership and sponsorship. The organization can capitalize buildings, purchase electronic medical record (EMR) systems, pool employees, and act as a supplier for equipment and other purchased goods. It can be owned by doctors or sponsored by a hospital.

Group Practice without Walls (GPWW)

A GPWW is typically a network of physicians who have merged into one legal entity but maintain individual practice locations and who distribute income through some kind of equation that concentrates on cost allocation. A great deal of autonomy is retained at each site, and the environment for the physician is pretty much unchanged. The central management owns equipment and hires staff and provides administrative services. This type of a group practice is not a true group in that it has a structure that prevents any active management of the physician environment to facilitate (or force) change. It was designed to get around contracting in states and under managed care scenarios where individual practices could not achieve any kind of contracting impact.

This type of entity is almost as inefficient as the messenger model, and it is also less attractive under modern interpretations of Stark laws since there are referral and ownership implications that reward a doctor for sending patients along a particular path for treatment. A practice structured in this form would be well advised to have a compensation plan that meets current compliance standards and has been reviewed by an experienced health care attorney. Since this model fails to achieve any form of efficiency and cannot easily contract on a group basis, its application is limited under emerging health care reform.

Group Practice

An "integrated" provider offers a comprehensive corporate umbrella for the management of a diversified health care delivery team. This could be a large group multispecialty practice of doctors, or it could include a hospital. It could include a number of hospitals and even a health plan of some kind. It would certainly encompass a variety of ancillary services and treatment centers. It has the capability to provide several levels of health care to patients in geographically contiguous areas. Physicians practice as employees of the system or in a tightly affiliated physician group.

This model, when mature, can contract in a variety of settings and in a various number of forms. Assuming that it has a market presence, it is a formidable negotiator for managed care companies, and it can command and deploy considerable resources and infrastructure to manage the components of health care access and care. The integrated delivery system has its own acronym—IDS. This is the present gold standard that most provider groups are trying to achieve.

Captive Physician Group

In the IDS definition, physicians fit in as employees, subcontractors, or in a group or group of groups. Sometimes this takes the form of a "captive" physicians corporation, or it could be a foundation model. These differ by corporate structure but not by form and intent. A captive is a for-profit corporation that is sponsored and supported by an IDS. A medical foundation has two components: the foundation itself, which is a not-for-profit, tax-exempt entity, and the physician group, which provides medical services under a professional services contract to the foundation. Under either form, the captive or the foundation, the parent acquires the business and clinical assets of a mid- to large-sized group practice, or it hires a doctor or providers. The parent corporation holds the provider number and conducts all business management aspects of the enterprise.

Another model that is prevalent, especially in larger teaching institutions, is the faculty practice model where a hospital-sponsored group functions to teach residents and house officers, and it generally provides services to the "unassigned patients" or clinic populations. It is worthy of mention since this is the model that may be a structure that needs to be combined with others in order for a hospital or health system to achieve a true market option under whatever forms may arise for contracting in the future.

Other Models and Combinations of Models

Any number of these approaches can be combined and modified to suit specific situations. Private practices, for example, can form an MSO to handle "back office" functions and be part of a PHO for some contracting and employ a messenger model for other contracting efforts. Other models include staff model HMO practices, captive (or sponsored) group practices that participate in IPAs, and new and emerging models that are connected with retail medical programs and direct employer managed health care practices. Each is an applied tool that is defined by the local contracting and historical professional relationships in a legal environment that has both national and state limitations.

Summary Issues

- No one model works in every situation or for every type of group.
- Each model has its own regulatory challenges.
- The transition from the present to the desired will take many steps, some of which may present the need to consider alternative models.
- All of the models need a basic infrastructure—contracting capability, coordination of billing, income determination processes, governance, and oversight.

Chapter 2

Does Anyone Know the Definition of Integration?

We probably have to view the concept of integration as scientists view things like black holes and quarks. Actually, they have definitions, but they have never seen either of these phenomena. They surmise what they are by observing factors in the known universe, and then they come up with a theorem that fits the measurements that they think are being caused by the quark (or the black hole or whatever). The same goes for integration in health care. Many moving parts in and around a hospital are either more coordinated or less. One health care system can judge its level of integration (coordination or efficiency?) against another. The friction from inefficiencies can be studied as well. The measures become the focus of discussion rather than the core principles.

True integration can only be achieved when the overall business enterprise can be managed like an Apple or a Google with one set of underlying principles and goals. The goals are known to every participant and manager, and they receive their bonuses as well as share exposure to any hazards that the business enterprise must face. Every factor of production and service is aligned in an overall search for stability, market cohesion, and growth. Each part of the organization supports other parts in order to assure its own survival and the long-term success of the corporation in which it operates.

Maybe, realizing that these business principles are not very achievable in the short term in health care, we should use a physicist's approach and just study what an organization that is integrated might look like to a consumer or to a factor of production connected with it (Figure 2.1).

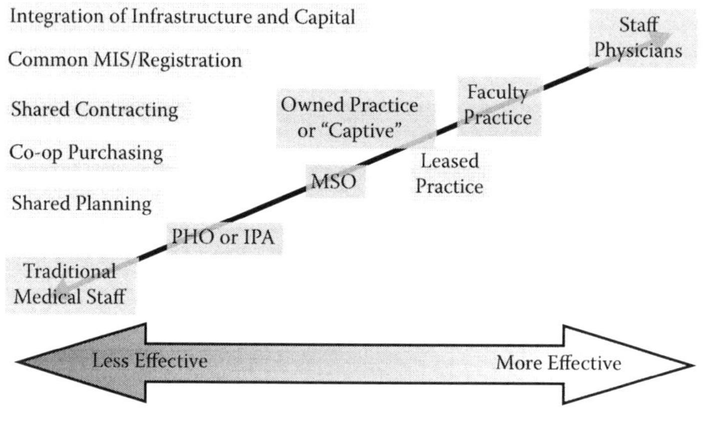

Figure 2.1 Integration at various stages.

How Will We Know If We Are Integrated? Maybe, We Already Are!

The consumer and the manager and the physician all approach, and are impacted by, factors of integration that can be easily described. These factors do not define integration, but they are definitely observations that are not common to most medical enterprises. They are, however, common to staff model HMOs and to established and mature group practices that have incorporated medical ancillaries within their service profile (think Kaiser and the Mayo Clinic). Each issue in this list is important to assess in the integration journey. It is either present and dependable or part of the planning process.*

1. Clinical data are reported on an individual basis and compared against group norms and national benchmarks.
2. A well-defined and published governance process addresses matters common to all sites and providers and employee groups.
3. Patient satisfaction and access tracking occur across all access sites.
4. Referral tracking is universal across all practice environments.
5. Universal registration, all practices, all sites.
6. Unified medical records and common forms for scripts, referral notes, progress notes, etc.
7. Common risk pools exist where possible and applicable.

* Lists and tables and examples from this book can be downloaded in updated and expanded format from the website www.medicalstaffintegration.org.

8. Practitioner reimbursement is related to performance, quality, and conformance to program objectives.
9. Group outcome indicators and individual performance rewarded as a function of outcome data.
10. Single answering service and coordinated patient scheduling—all offices, all sites.
11. Policies and procedures consistent for all sites. Standards for employee policies and job descriptions are the same site to site.
12. Mid-level providers (if used) are credentialed at the same level and operating from group-defined protocols.
13. Establishment of group-wide standards for use of ancillaries, imaging, rehab, etc.
14. Common protocols for admissions, discharge planning, patient recall, etc.
15. Common purchasing procedures and the application of common supply items.
16. Common computer and management information systems (MIS).
17. Defined group governance processes that address efficiency, quality, and integration as core values.
18. A commonly applied set of standards for all professional and support staff (including doctors) relating to aspects of continuing education.
19. The development of coordinated coverage programs in areas of need that might involve staff or doctors from a variety of offices.
20. The development of commonly agreed upon patient care plans, best practices methodologies, etc.
21. Common financial reporting standards such as collection rules, chart of accounts, write-off procedures, indigent care policies, etc.
22. All providers are engaged in all managed care contracts and payer programs accepted by the group. Single signature contracting through a representative who acts on behalf of the entire group.
23. Established standards exist for related support groups (emergency department, anesthesiologists, or radiologists).

The list could go on and on, but the reader can be pretty well assured that if the answer to most, or all, of the statements is positive, he or she is in a country with universal health care or in an Army hospital. These are not commonly achieved standards except in the most integrated of environments, and these standards can be used to confirm the existence of an integrated health care system even when there is argument over the basic definition.

Integration Is Not a Place, It Is a Process

The idea of integration and the way that the idea is applied are important to distinguish. The race toward integration is one that has two contestants with very different tools and many objectives along the way that might be an advantage for one and an impediment for the other. One should reflect on the reality show *The*

Amazing Race and then on the folktale about John Brown and his hammer vs. the steam-powered pile driver. The payers, Medicare and self-funded businesses and consumers, are rushing toward contracts that are more well defined and all-inclusive. They are looking for a true marketplace where value can be defined and where price is transparent. Except for the fact that there is some unintended cost shifting as publicly funded needs constrain market responses, the goals are similar and the mid-state objectives overlap. Overall, the payers and consumers are looking for a new way to buy and consume health care services.

The providers, hospitals, and physicians are moving in the same direction, but each has a differing view of the end objective and competing mid-state objectives. In most cases, these partnerships are internally competitive and the parties are generally trying to have minimal changes in the way that health care is priced and resources are deployed. The providers are used to the status quo, and any change that is implemented is generally unwelcome since it generates additional cost and risk, but seldom with any improvement in unit or total revenues.

The payers would like to contract with a staff model HMO,* and the providers would like to continue their disintegrated delivery of piecemeal products and services. Integration represents a costly political and financial process.

One can assume that the payers will prevail and that the providers will be moving in any number of ways from the present state to one that more efficiently is able to contract in a post-PPACA (Patient Protection and Affordable Care Act) world. At least that is the premise on which this book is written. The next assumption is that they will do so in a variety of ways, many of which may be inefficient and costly. The end goal may not be achieved in a way that is very pretty, but if the market moves in the direction that the payers want, the hospitals and doctors will get there eventually. Hopefully, some of the ideas in this book will outline some of the hazards to avoid in the journey.

The form of final organization will take one of two paths: central governance of a combined and unified organization where everyone has common goals and well-understood objectives† or a governance model that is based upon a variety

* HMOs are generally well understood. A health maintenance organization (HMO) is one that can assume the entire cost (and all risk) for the health care for an individual or a group. A staff model HMO is one that does so with a team of doctors that are on staff, hired rather than contracted. This is the Kaiser model that has thrived since it was introduced and refined in the early 1950s.

† The reader should think of organizations like the Mayo Clinic and Kaiser. These are organizations with a long history of integrated design, each of which has sophisticated models for the inclusion of physicians in the governance process.

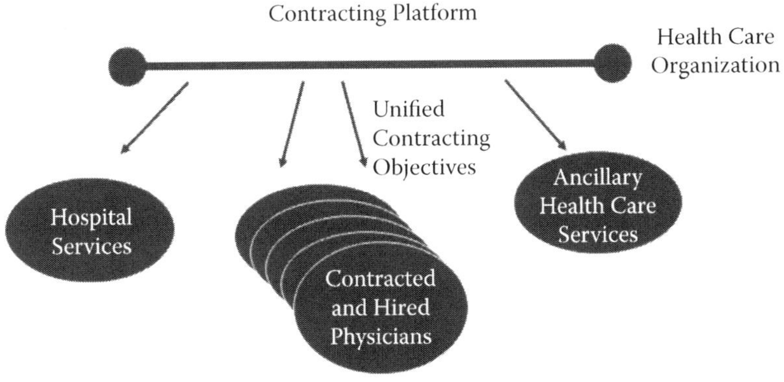

Figure 2.2 The ideal contracting structures depending upon who controls the platform.

of contractual relationships that are monitored and reorganized and restructured based upon the currently prevailing market and regulatory environments.*

Providers think of achieving the former (complete and seamless integration) but will get there using the latter (multiple contractual and a variety of business relationships). Figure 2.2 represents the ideal arrangement.

However, seldom is the ideal immediately achievable, and Figure 2.3 represents the situation that is often attempted by health care systems and their partner physicians while working toward the ideal as they construct a variety of interim organizations.

The attempt to maintain some semblance of the status quo in a rapidly changing reimbursement and regulatory environment is often the desired goal that is a driving force in the development of the interim organization. This is a common planning mistake that may result in the combination of problems shown in Figure 2.4.

The problem is obvious and the solutions are not. The goals of maintaining the status quo while moving to a new type of reimbursement may have challenges that many systems cannot face, and the result, for some of them, will be catastrophic. This may be a reason that there are so many health care consolidation events and

* For some providers, there is also the need to be current with the state health care environment since some states, like Massachusetts, have moved in a direction that is on a different trajectory than the national programming. Also, some states have regulatory environments that are more, or less, conducive to some of the ideas reflected in the common lexicon of physician-hospital relationships.

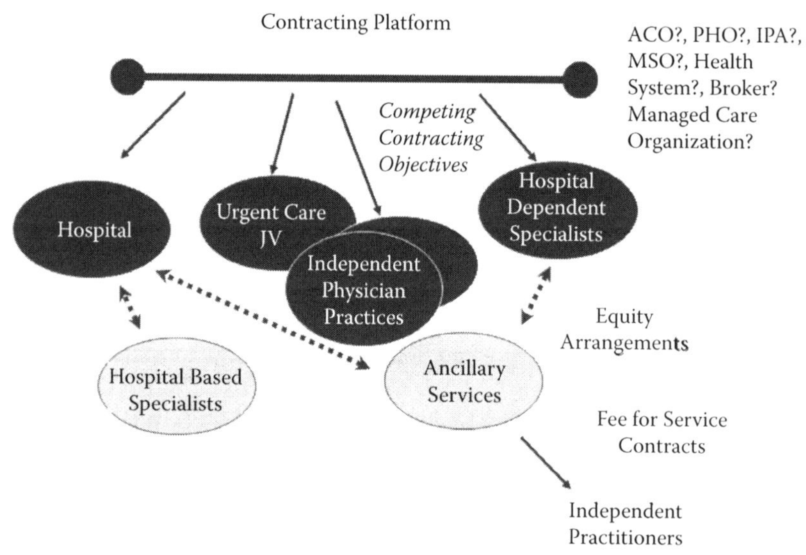

Figure 2.3 Desired state hospital/physician platform.

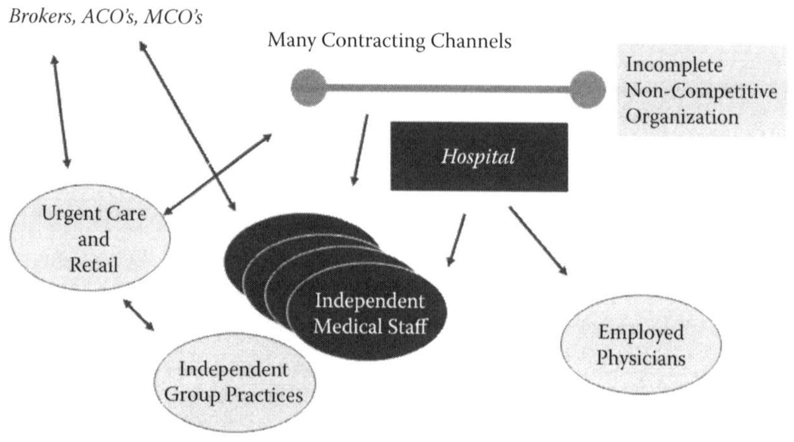

Figure 2.4 Present state contracting format.

bankruptcies.[*] The future is not going to be a simple reorganization of the organizations of the past.

Integration and the Challenges of Income Determination

Doctors, whether employed or contracted, can be part of the integration effort as long as they have contracts and their income is determined in some fashion that is aligned with the governance and goals of the business enterprise. This is one of those simple statements that is hard to implement in a programmatic sense and which assumes that the term *doctors* is a universal descriptor.

This does not mean that physicians cannot be motivated by other issues and principles, but it does mean that if a system is to be built that is dependable, it has to be built upon some kind of basic economics and defined financial relationships. The doctors may have taken the same oath that was shared by the Mayo brothers and Albert Schweitzer, but the Mayos eventually built their program into a major medical complex that is known around the world, while Dr. Schweitzer earned a Nobel Peace Prize. Most hospitals emulate the Mayo model, and most doctors think of themselves as carrying on the tradition of Dr. Schweitzer. Generally, they are both striving for something that is not attainable.

The Mayos and the good Dr. Schweitzer were not really contemporaries, but they came from the same general era. They entered medicine as it was changing from an art to a science and gaining respect in an environment where there was no defined or organized reimbursement channel. These physicians were not concerned as much about regulatory and financial matters, and none of them had contracted patient bases or payer intermediaries with which to contend. They also did not have much in the way of technology, and they did not have practices that would be considered particularly capital-intensive. The present-day physician is entering a different world, and one in which his or her behavior is being channeled by the necessity to address financial constraints, regulatory hurdles, and market barriers that would have baffled Will and Charlie Mayo.

It is estimated that the average graduating physician is now carrying in the neighborhood of $200,000 in debt.[†] This means that he or she cannot purchase a

---

[*] The American Bankruptcy Institute has a health care committee that tracks such events on an informal basis as well as physician bankruptcies. Anecdotal evidence is all that is available since institutions move in and out of bankruptcy situations and many reported bankruptcies are simply a prelude to a takeover or merger. Also, with a physician practice, as with any business, a bankruptcy may be a tool that simply signals a restructuring of assets.

[†] Association of American Medical Colleges, Trends in Cost and Debt at U.S. Medical Schools Using a New Measure of Medical School Cost of Attendance, Briefing Volume 12, Number 2, July 2012.

traditional practice and probably cannot afford to start his or her own. The present physician population is emerging with the rest of the country from a recession that has impacted their personal net worth and their retirement funds, and they have not only lost equity in their homes, but if they own their practice, they also are probably not going to be able to find a buyer among today's crop of graduating physicians.

Enter the hospital that is now alert to the need to create a network of providers who can be more dependable and collaborate on a higher plane than the traditional medical staff. The doctors need capital and the hospital has it, or at least has access to it. This has caused the marketplace for practice acquisitions to heat up at a time when there are still many traditional structures in place that are operating on a parallel basis as contracting mechanisms. Private fee-for-service medicine is now competing in an environment with contracting organizations whose members are slowly (in some cases quickly) reorganizing themselves in different forms that might make these organizations history. They are exploring new relationships, but sometimes they are using outmoded contracting technology.

Summary Issues

- Every organization is using terminology related to integration without being integrated.
- Doctors are moving away from traditional private practice, and this trend is fueled by hospitals, capital needs, and reimbursement changes.
- Few organizations are abandoning their present structures as they create new ones.
- The technology of contracting between doctors and hospitals is outmoded.

Chapter 3

Does What We Have Now Actually Work?

The simple answer is probably not. The more complete answer is that the physician-hospital organization (PHO) or independent provider association (IPA) or management services organization (MSO) or whatever interim structure that exists now is probably inadequate for the needs of future contracting adventures. If the traditional hospital and medical staff structure worked, most hospitals would never have capitalized these alternative forms of hospital-physician partnerships. The traditional medical staff did not fulfill the need to be able to contract with the managed care forms emerging in the 1980s and 1990s, and the present partnerships won't handle the population management* challenges of the present and the near term. This book will cover these forms, but only because they are part of the reorganization process, and they are not going away soon. They may not be structured correctly for the future, but the medical staff is not going to disappear, and neither are the networks that have been created around them. Figure 3.1 displays the various types of physician relationships that a hospital may have to organize in order to respond to a contracting opportunity (or threat). The typical contracting group is an IPA or a PHO, but that may only contain part of the medical staff, and it might

* Most of the present platforms for contracting will be based on the management of populations rather than patients. This is a relatively new combination of words that is equivalent in a relative sense to capitation where the health system is contracted on a global fee basis to supply all of the health care needs for the defined population under a contract.

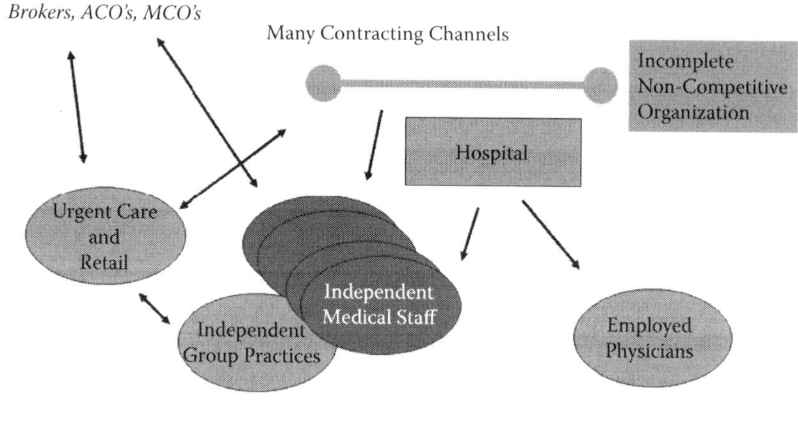

Figure 3.1 Physicians can contract through many channels.

also include others in the community that are not within the traditional medical staff. Contracted and employed physicians are always in the contracting group.*

Figure 3.2 is a depiction of a "universe" of providers that reflects the challenge that a hospital might have with delivering care to a patient population when the basic physician complement is arrayed in a number of different relationships, not all of them supportive.

How Did We Get Here? How Do We Get Where We Need to Be?

The typical consultative response is: "It all depends." There is no reason to study why a system exists unless one is a historian or a medical sociologist. The most notable was Odin W. Anderson,† who taught at the University of Chicago and who summarized all health care systems as being composed of a system of scientists and caregivers no matter what the payment modality. Hospitals, in his experience, were a secondary issue. The scientist component would be equivalent to our notion of

* Contracted physicians should be in the group that the hospital uses to contract with outside payers, but anesthesiologists and radiologists and others might actually elect to be independent of any contracting efforts even though they depend upon the hospital for their basic patient bases.

† Dr. Anderson was a prolific author and student of health care systems around the world. At the height of his career, he dedicated a portion of each year to live in a different country to study its health care delivery system at all levels.

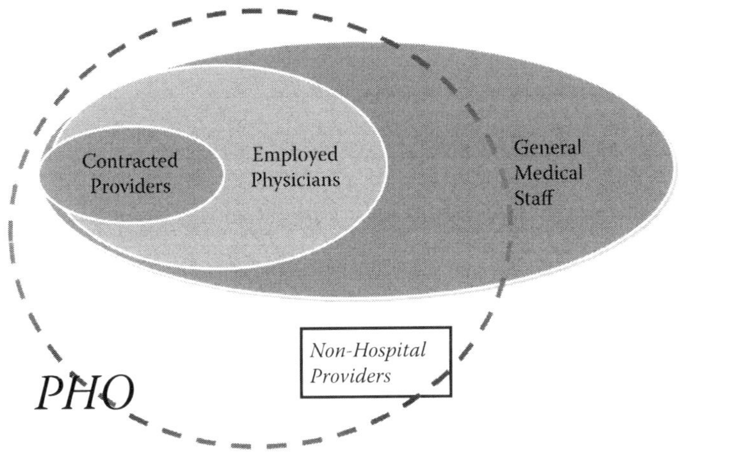

Figure 3.2 The PHO is seldom exclusive enough to be effective.

a physician or that person who directs and manages the care, and the caregivers would be the people who provide support during the healing process. These simple building blocks are found in every system of care, and they are only confused and compounded by the way society reimburses the various classes of providers.

How we got to where we are and how any health care system is designed is less important than where it is going and how it will take that journey. Most hospitals and health systems are founded on community property that was once donated to a nonprofit or charitable organization, and it operated on donations and on payments from a variety of sources. Technology was not a factor since high-tech did not exist and pharmacological remedies were unproven and unpredictable. Present health care systems morphed over the years into complex organizations under a variety of payment systems and technological advances to now be a form that is very capital-intensive and financially sophisticated. Doctors have emerged as sophisticated medical scientists and, because of the fee-for-service health system, sometimes as entrepreneurs. The near-term future suggests that their involvement in the business side of medicine may be on the wane as hospitals and health systems purchase practices and employ physicians to create a system that can respond to the many new pressures of the Patient Protection and Affordable Care Act (PPACA) and related consumer demand. Essentially, hospitals are moving to formal integration that bypasses many of the formats that have been traditionally used as stepping-stones and moving to an employment model. This is at a time when physicians are discovering that their practices are undercapitalized and, in some cases, undermanaged and understaffed to be able to compete in what they correctly think will be a tsunami of regulatory and bureaucratic processes.

Physicians are anxious to sell and hospitals are anxious to buy in a competitive marketplace that is undergoing rapid change. For the health care institution, this presents both a hazard and an opportunity. The same goes for the doctors. Long term this transformation may work out well for everyone. Patients will be served by an integrated health care enterprise. Physicians can concentrate on medicine and not on the complexities of business management and capital formation. Hospitals, at least the ones that survive, will be managing from a consolidated platform that includes all aspects of the health care delivery model.

Near term, the question is how to construct the structures and transactions that can allow the transformation to occur smoothly and without any unfortunate and unintended consequences. The health care industry experienced a similar spate of practice sales in the early and mid-1990s, and the result was generally a failure for all concerned.*

What Is Different This Time? What Is the Same?

The assumptions under which an MSO or a PHO† development occurs generally are that the organization will provide superior management and external contracting opportunities for physician members, and that the organization can operate with some level of efficiency and, eventually, justify its own existence as a standalone operation. However, actual experience varies, and the environments in which a practice operates simply do not stay stable. Over time, most physician organizations find themselves in a situation that requires a reorganization of goals and objectives and a reevaluation of their basic reason for existence.

These things do not fix themselves. Performance must be reviewed, and the structure and governance processes that led to whatever deficiencies exist (or are perceived to exist) must be corrected. The following outline suggests an approach to evaluating MSO/PHO operations in order to suggest a method for changing their structure and systems to assure compliance with either the original objectives under

* This set of "unfortunate and unintended consequences" included not only doctors and hospitals but also investors. The most profound case study was that of PHYCOR, one of the many physician practice management companies that emerged to capitalize upon the practice consolidation trend only to discover that the metrics of most deals did not make good business sense. The impact of this miscalculation on one community in Michigan was detailed by *Medical Economics*, writing about the destruction of the Burns Clinic and the challenges to the community it served. Anita J. Slomski, After Playing with Fire, This Group Went Down in Flames, *Medical Economics*, September 6, 1999, http://medicaleconomics.modernmedicine.com/medical-economics/news/clinical/pediatrics/after-playing-fire-group-went-down-flames.

† This section will reference the MSO and the PHO since they are the typical structures in which hospitals form partnerships with doctors. However, the same format can be used for an IPA or IPO review.

which they were formed or their capability to address the new challenges that their members and investors now face.

Review original business plans, projections, goals, objectives, etc., to determine the overall structure of the MSO/PHO and the intent of its founders. Where such goals or plans are internally inconsistent, identify whatever might have been unreasonable or overly optimistic. Before wondering about the present status of the organization, it is helpful to ask why it originally existed in the first place. Once this exercise is complete, one must review present operational structures against industry standards and marketplace alternatives to define the optimum level of performance that must be achieved for the present mix of clients and services. What does the organization need to be able to accomplish now?

Is the structure itself outmoded? Review the contractual relationships between equity participants (owners) and the MSO/PHO. Review the contracts that exist between the entity and the client base. Define the legal responsibilities of all parties and compare that legal orientation to practical and political realities existing between the client physicians and the equity holders. Is the organization structured properly for the business challenges in the present marketplace? If services are part of the portfolio, assess their profile and analyze each service relative to the efficiency of that service and how it stacks up against competition. Does the organization earn its customers or are they merely present because of tradition and peer pressure? Are we really serving the doctors in any unique way?

Review the communications that have been shared with clients/physicians to understand clearly the level of expectations that might be reasonably held relating to the MSO/PHO and its member benefits. Develop an interview process that can determine the attitudes of existing clients/physicians while ascertaining their need (and perceived need) for additional services. What do the doctors think is necessary in this market and in the foreseeable future? These surveys have to be conducted in a way that will reflect a practical need and not the hopes of the clients. Doctors may wish for the organization to do things that are impractical or impossible, and a survey process must work to determine actual needs and not philosophical desires.

Assess each contract (or business function) on a stand-alone basis and develop a customer ranking on the basis of profitability (or potential profitability) and the general level of satisfaction, including some commentary on the likelihood of client conversion or improvement.

Review resource allocation and operational processes to determine whether internal efficiencies might be gained by some kind of reengineering. The last step is to compile material from the financial and program audit, the customer interviews, the service and contract comparative analysis, and any historical or functional information into some form of a present status report on the MSO/PHO that concentrates upon the continuation of service or the feasibility of transforming the organization into one that can be meaningful in the near-term future.

Was the organization, in hindsight, founded upon sound principles and assumptions? Do the present services compete successfully in the local marketplace for services the physicians could simply buy from a competitor or provide for themselves? Is the organization structured to be able to make decisions effectively and, once made, implement them? Can the organization expect to maintain its contracts and client base beyond the present relationships? Can the organization reasonably be expected to attract additional members in its present form?

Are there structural opportunities for the organization to reorganize its equity or its governance to be able to improve the relationship with its clients by including them at different and various levels of the decision-making process? What goals or objectives of the organization are internally competitive or inconsistent? How can these be resolved? What additional investment must be dedicated to the organization MSO to achieve the results that are necessary for effectiveness? What resources exist that must be reorganized to achieve program and system goals? Who should do what to assure program success? What is a reasonable timeline for change?

A report is not implementation. This exercise is one that is meant to "clear the air" over existing structures and remove (or repair) any structure that does not allow the enterprise, the health care system, and its committed doctor-partners, to move aggressively forward. Often, it is more efficient to move to a new structure of some kind than to depend upon one that is redundant or inefficient or, worse, unable to be governed. If there is a feeling of some kind that the present organization is functioning appropriately, it must be able to have (at the least) single-signature contracting capability. It has to be able to contract in new and innovative ways. It needs to be in a position to manage capitation and bundled pricing contracts that include both doctor and hospital services. These are challenging to any organization, let alone one that is comprised of physicians and a hospital.

Same Players, Traditional Structures, New Tools

The participants in the game are the same and the environment and the rules are pretty much the same. However, the tools are different. There is also a very different audience. The pressures are more acute and there are some additional factors—like consumerism and retail health outlets. The systems are now more likely to come to the table armed with data from sophisticated medical records systems and data exchanges. They now have experience with both managed care and the ownership and management of physician practices. This does not mean that they now know what they need to do and how to do it, but it does mean that they are more cautious and that they now know what *not* to do.

Add to this intuitive and cautious landscape a heavier dose of regulation and the scene is set for a much more fierce and technologically driven engagement with added stakeholders and combatants. This will lead, and already has, to different types of alliances and collaborations and a more costly process but more rapid transition. Transactions are only part of the process. They are an event, and doctors and hospitals know how to conduct themselves through this first part of the process. Many transactions are structured to hamper the transitional period following the actual corporate or legal reorganization. Many are also going to be conducted in the shadow, and within structures that are still in place and which have more limited scope. The following chapters will address these factors and give the reader some references on new ways to deal with historical structures.

Summary Issues

- Most existing organizations cannot make decisions effectively and efficiently.
- Seldom can traditional organizations audit themselves and change membership as necessary to compete in a changing marketplace.
- Few organizations possess the data or the infrastructure necessary to assess performance that is truly driven by quality measures.

Chapter 4

Ignoring Fundamentals Will Produce Unwanted Results

In Chapter 2, several questions were asked regarding the basic functioning of the group that is being used for implementing whatever integration strategy is underway. Often, the group was defined and designed under a different, less intense, form of competition. It is helpful to review some basic principles or ideals that a group might consider in the present environment. The following points are offered for consideration. They simply state what a contracting organization that provides services has to achieve in order to compete with the various accountable care organizations (ACOs) and insurance exchanges that will be contracting for their services.

This organization must have a mechanism to monitor and impact change among its members based upon quality measures.

The organization has to function to assure that data are available across its membership and throughout its contracting cycle.

This process will probably show that the physician-hospital organization (PHO)/ management services organization (MSO) has been operating simply because it exists and, like many organizations, without an overall plan. When an organization fails to plan, it is often surprised by how quickly the marketplace becomes transformed and how quickly it can become irrelevant. Actually, most reevaluation processes really are an effort to define a plan that was either originally ill-conceived or which was not kept up to date.

Frankly, if these questions cannot be answered positively, the enterprise should seriously consider either ignoring or sidelining the PHO or MSO or independent provider association (IPA) or whatever the organization is that it had originally chartered. Long ago, most hospitals began to ignore the traditional medical staff structures and created new ones. Now it is time to recognize that these new organizations may need to be relegated to social structures, and that business investment and capital may need to be channeled into new forms of physician partnerships.

The acquisition or reorganization of a physician practice is done, in some cases, in a hurry. It should never be done without having a basic premise related to the overall goals of the health care institution. A *premise* is another word for a *plan*, and a plan takes some time and effort to put together. Many hospitals are now, like they did in the mid-1990s, buying practices because that is what is being done by their competitors or because the doctor is on the doorstep. This will work out for many institutions badly because they will have acquired the wrong practices for the wrong reason and in a format that is unsustainable.

Planning might not be a process that thrives in a foxhole, but there are always some fundamentals that are agreed upon before armed units are sent into the field with weapons and ammunition. Developing a physician network should have the same level of attention. Some practices might be needed and some not. Some can be purchased or leased, and some can be contracted in other ways. This is a question of the strategic value of the practice and its nature and composition. The simple question of capital constraint might define the process. If there are any number of practices that need to "partner," and capital is limited, does the hospital want to contract (buy, lease, collaborate) with the best of them or with the most desperate? Hopefully, the question is one that is asked and answered before even one transaction is engaged, but at whatever the stage the hospital finds itself, planning and ranking opportunities is better earlier than later.

Different Practices, Different Relationships, Different Approaches

Different types of physicians and different types of physician groups must be addressed with unique tools. A hospital or a health care system craves standardization. So does the military, but it long ago recognized that there are different branches of the services, and categories like the Coast Guard and the Marines have different roles and operate in different environments. However, when the nation is at war, they are managed by a central authority that is comprised of a "committee" called the Joint Chiefs of Staff. In wartime, and when multiple countries have

Table 4.1 Physicians Have Differing Needs and Characteristics

Hospital based and hospital dependent	Emergency room physicians Anesthesiologists Radiologists Pathologists Intensivists Hospitalists
Capital-intensive and independent	Ophthalmologists Plastic surgeons Orthopods
Capital-intensive and dependent	Cardiologists Nephrologists Obstetricians Urologists Oncologists
Non-capital-intensive specialist	General surgeons Dermatologists Internal medicine specialists (pulmonology, GI)
Primary care	Family practitioners Pediatricians

agreed upon a single objective or enemy, there is a supreme commander in chief of some kind.

Whatever the health care system wants to call its coordinating committee, it will almost certainly include administration and the key stakeholder representatives of the most prominent and powerful branches of the services. Like the various sources of manpower drawn upon by a nation at war, there may be citizen soldiers, or in the case of the health care system, the members of the private attending medical staff (noncontracted and independent) may be pressed into service. The traditional groupings from which the resources of a medical staff are formed and deployed, like the field forces of an army, need to be categorized and understood. Generally, they can be described in a few distinct categories, and each category can be understood by the market forces that impact it. Table 4.1 reflects one type of categorization process that might be used as a starting point for planning and for the development of a better understanding of how to address the channels of influence that a health care system can use to influence different types of physician groups.

Academic Practices

The previous section mentioned academic practices, which are often governed by their own set of rules and standards. Many of the principles outlined in this book still apply, but the academic practice has a separate set of guidelines that must be addressed, or at least cannot be ignored. The academic practice implies teaching, and teaching means residents, house officers, and other health care providers in a variety of observation and caregiver roles. The academic standards will be defined by a specialty organization with its own set of guidelines and markers, the most important of which will have to underlie any contracting or management process.

These academic requirements are loosely organized to deploy care to clinic populations and to train new physicians. Their existence is sometimes dictated by the needs of a self-funded (uninsured) community of patients and by the dictates of a training program that has both inefficient delivery models (students and their physician-instructors) and an additional set of regulations (educational certification bodies). These are not in any way statements of judgment or critique—just facts that the hospital and health system must address as part of the overall plan. Adding to the positive side of the balance sheet is the fact that these programs also command additional Medicare funding in the form of graduate medical education support, but these funds themselves are often not enough to justify a program that does not otherwise have its own strategic position within the health care delivery matrix.

Academic practices also have another major component—academics. This is not a trite statement; this is an observation that demands special care in the development of a financial structure that includes teaching programs with substantial full-time and voluntary physicians. They participate, but at a cost. Their time is focused on the educational process, and they may not be motivated to provide the most efficient care. They also have the moral high ground in most discussions that address quality. The phrase "town vs. gown" also comes to mind since it was coined to describe the tension that exists between private attending medical staff and those salaried physicians who move in a different world and who can often command more of an institution's resources since they are "teaching."

Retail-Oriented Practices

There are any number of practices that orient themselves directly to the retail marketplace. These are fostered by giants like Walgreens and Walmart and CVS. Each is hiring and placing mid-level providers and primary care providers in close

Figure 4.1 Hospitals and pharmacies collaborate for different reasons.

proximity to other services such as pharmacy and optical and consumer health care products. They offer a limited menu of services at a definitive price level, generally on a cash-only basis.

These practitioners cannot contract directly with local health care systems, but some will be involved with a hospital and on its medical staff. However, the health care system cannot ignore this trend, and there must be a link in some way to the contracting level that can assure a formal working relationship. Actually, this is harder than it sounds since the major corporations that sponsor these services are national, and hospitals are generally local or regional (Figure 4.1).

Concierge Practices and Aesthetic-Oriented Practices

These practices have a connection directly to the consumer marketplace. One might argue that practices like plastic surgery aesthetic practices and cosmetic dermatologists should not be lumped in with primary care "concierge-style" practices, but both categories are moving outside the normal reimbursement structure to capture specific segments of the patients who can afford to pay for their own care. They confuse the marketplace somewhat because seldom are these practices only serving direct-pay patients. Often they serve multiple categories of patients, and contracting with them can be a challenge because the norms of the practice cannot be judged against those of most practices in a marketplace, and there are almost no national norms against which they can be reviewed.

Just as Walgreens and CVS are developing retail offerings at the "sidewalk level" of health care, there are firms that are developing what they label as higher-end services and enlisting physicians to their camps. Examples would include the many national vision correction firms and plastic surgery service firms such as LifeStyle Lift™ and Sono Bello™. Each is an organization that devotes much of its resources to channeling consumers through advertising and around conventional referral channels. There is no national leader in the concierge industry as yet, but several firms are trying to gain a trade or brand presence by signing up patients and their doctors in a simultaneous reach for the consumer market.

These firms are fueled by consumers who have a ready bank of dollars to be spent on elective procedures in funds that have been created by high-deductible insurance programs that encourage the consumers to save or warehouse some dollars in health care savings accounts that are not taxable. These funds are theoretically for covering high deductibles and increasingly more expensive co-pays, but when they are sitting in a savings account without an immediate purpose, they may also be used for liposuction or vision correction.

Practices that fall into this category include dermatology, cosmetic plastic surgery, sports medicine (orthopedics), ophthalmology (retail eyewear and vision correction surgery), oral surgery, etc. In some cases, other product lines may blur the distinctions within these arenas. Examples might be the treatment of erectile dysfunction, hormonal therapy, psychiatry, integrative medicine, cosmetic vascular surgery, etc.

Hospital-Based and Codependent Practices

Most health care systems ignore the power of referrals and exclusive contracting and rely upon contracts and cash to channel physician behavior. The power of awarding a continuous stream of referrals or allowing a physician group some level of exclusivity or primacy in scheduling has not been well used by hospitals, mostly because they do not consider these relationship and structural factors to have value because they have never attempted to cash it in. A standard business would recognize the overt and implied consideration that is under its control and trade it for some kind of return. Hospitals should be reviewing all contracts and franchises and exclusive relationships and ask themselves the following questions:

When was the last time we did a complete review on the service that is being provided by the ABC group?

Does the ABC group regularly and routinely support our programming?

What referral channels does the ABC group derive through its exclusive relationship that we need to count and control?

Do we have a formal contract that is functional under the emerging health care scenario? That is, can we contract on behalf of this group? Can we exchange information effectively with them? Can we incorporate their contribution to care within our quality and value-based offerings?

Does this group have the endorsement of our medical staff?

Is this group part of, or supportive of, our defined narrow network of specialty groups that we can depend upon for risk contracting, development processes, joint ventures, etc.?

Physicians in Different Disciplines Have Differing Needs

Table 4.1 suggests that some practitioners have a classification that is somewhat formed by their specialty and its need for certain resources.

One can certainly argue with the choice of which box contains each category of physician specialty, but the exercise is really to think about doctors as falling into categories. Once that premise is accepted, the health care system and its administrative team can fashion responses that are more tailored to the needs of each specialty group. This approach to categorizing is not meant to be one that allows pigeonholing, but one that promotes some thinking about how doctors relate to a hospital. This changes over time, as one can see, with the emergence of hospitalists and their support for primary care practices. In the 1970s and 1980s one would assume that a doctor with a community-based practice needed access to hospital beds and the patient admitting privileges that go with them. With the advent of a hospitalist program, that doctor's relationship with the hospital has changed. If a doctor feels that staff privileges are important, it is generally because the physician wants to be on the hospital's "find-a-doctor" website, rather than to care for inpatients.

Accepting that this categorization system is general and rather simplistic, we can ignore for a moment the specialty categories and ask what the integration methodologies might be for the general categories. Hospitals have resources, and linking with physicians in a formal way implies using those resources in a judicious and efficient fashion. How these resources are used can be often defined by what each physician group needs. Table 4.2 suggests that goals vary by broad physician categories.

Of course, the size of the hospital and the size and nature of the group might dictate different approaches. Academics might also be a factor. If the categories listed above seem either a little simplistic or overly complex, it is because the reader is judging them by his or her own environment and background. That is the point. One should consider the health care system and develop a strategy for the classes and categories of physicians and practitioners that operate within it.

Table 4.2 Integration Form Must Match Physician Characteristics

	Physician Needs	*Health System Goals*	*Integration*
Hospital based/ dependent	Hospital exclusive franchise; controlled patient flow	Quality and coverage assurances and minimal subsidies; guaranteed access; acceptable behavior	Exclusive contract
Capital-intensive and independent	Access to primary care referrals and appropriate technology; linkage to product line support and hospital brand	Predictable consumer base and product line linkages; assurance of access; ability to measure and promote quality	Control the product line and referral sources; control access to the health system brand
Capital-intensive and dependent	Facility and program access; control of technology; access to an inpatient services unit	Predictable consumer base and product line linkages; assurance of access; ability to measure and promote quality	Control of access to technology and programming; joint ventures
Non-capital-intensive	Referrals from any source	Participation in network channels and assurance of access; patient admissions	Control the network access and channels of referrals
Primary care	Income stability and control over risk; access to emerging pricing and contracting models	Patient referrals to hospital-linked specialists; assurance of access; ability to predict quality	Equity participation

Summary Issues

- Most hospitals have a generic approach for addressing physician integration issues. This is a mistake that ignores potential resources for the sake of politics.
- The medical staff no longer define the gateway to the hospital. There are consumers and providers that are making the process of planning more complex as they develop their own unique primary care relationships with patients.
- Specialists are not all equal. Successful hospitals will need to know more about their specialist population and have more control over their behavior in the future as contracting begins to become more complex.

Chapter 5

Where Are We Headed and What Will Get Us There?

If what we have is not working, we need to think of what will work. The premise of this book is all about transforming the practice and engaging the traditional physicians practice in a manner that will complement the future contracting models that are now under development. The process is akin to the idea of forming a team that can go "where the puck is going" rather than where it has been.*

The other challenge is to be able to serve the increased demand that will be coming from all fronts through the Patient Protection and Affordable Care Act (PPACA). Some estimates are placed at or around an additional 40 million people moving from some kind of uninsured or underinsured state to coverage plans that will be mandatory. These are people who are going to be entering an already overcrowded health care system. Managing access and triage will become a critical part of each administrator's job description.

The questions may not be, "When can the doctor see me?" but "Can I get in?" The answer may soon depend upon how the contracts with the doctors have been arranged and how effectively the medical staff has been deployed (Figure 5.1).

Health care is going to a version of quality contracting combined with a dose of consumerism and more precise networks. This means that things like narrow networks and value-based networks will emerge. This is the form that must be

* Hopefully, the reader will recognize this saying as a quote from Wayne Gretzky, who stated such when he was asked what made him such a great hockey player.

Figure 5.1 Is this the health care marketplace under an additional 40 million citizens with health coverage?

anticipated by hospitals and doctors that are combining forces to face the new marketplace. The "narrow network" is a "select network," and it is defined by a group that is a subset of some other form of employee-wide, contact-wide, all-inclusive preferred provider organization (PPO) or managed care network of physicians and providers that has been precontracted to accept health care consumers at a negotiated fee structure. The selection of a subset of providers can be based upon several criteria:

- Quality or reputation of the provider
- A guarantee of timely access
- Adherence to defined access protocols for the population
- Integration with the central medical record system
- Involvement (credentialing) of the medical staff of the select hospitals in the system
- Compliance with "care management" or other protocols
- Utilization of other care resources related to the network, such as imaging and diagnostic programs
- Coordination of off-hours services with established call coverage groups

The idea that this is all about cost is missing the points related to access, value, and patient satisfaction. A case could be made that the specialist involved in this type of a program could actually be paid more if he or she assisted with ready access and monitored duplicative diagnostics and avoided wasteful duplicative events. Best practices in this arena could have a substantial positive effect on the projected cost savings or cost avoidance, but this program has to be developed, managed, and maintained in order to be effective. When the hospital enters into arrangements with doctors in the present environment, it is in anticipation of this type of a structure.

Simply put, the hospital can either participate in someone else's network or create its own. If it creates its own, then it has to have relevance in the local marketplace—to payers and consumers. This relevance is generally judged by whether the institution can command a profile of patients that can be organized through its own network of providers in a contract with one of the agents of change that are emerging under the PPACA or through employer coalitions.

Case Management and Care Management—The New Paradigm

It is important to note that there is a new term introduced in this chapter that bears definition beyond that which can be contained in a footnote. That is *care management*, which is an expansion of the idea of traditional case management. The concept of case management is not new. Most managed care programs have some form of a case manager that will intervene in an admission and perform some sort of secondary review and monitor the process related to a procedure to encourage efficient utilization of resources (or at least avoid waste, if possible). The care management function that is anticipated here is one that is population specific and directed to support only the components of the specific practice, employer, or beneficiary pool. It is case management that is directed to a particular part of the health care delivery profile.

The reason to note it here is that the newly designed practice will be incorporating care management within its infrastructure and assuring access to care managers from other environments. This can only be done with some kind of articulation with a medical record that is connected to performance standards and best practices protocols. Again, this begs the need for a structure that is well capitalized and well organized.

Care management is very involved and focused, and the care manager moves a patient from provider to provider, especially in a surgical event or an admission, with precision and knowledge of the local resources available. It extends and supports primary care, and it becomes an ally to the hospitalized individual and an advocate for the person in need of care. Once it is established and it has a "face," the patients will come to see it as a service and not a case management type of barrier to care.

The main areas of care management focus are:

Prevention of unnecessary admissions
Attention to admissions to assure that they are organized and efficient

Support of patients in making decisions that direct them toward more effective and more efficient providers
Prevention of unnecessary and duplicative testing
Prevention of unnecessary ED visits
Assessment of "best and most optimum" care locations (hospital, home, or extended care facility)
Assistance to patients in the consideration and evaluation of health service options, and how and when they are necessary
Provision of health coaching support to frequent health system users (the frequent fliers)
Development of relationships with providers to assure immediate access and timely reporting processes

This concept of care management is still under development. It can emerge as a function that is called a health care navigator or a health coach or any number of advisory-style facilitators. There is a growing movement for managed care organizations to employ these patient support functions, and there is also a trend to embed them within primary care practices, and they are even being employed in the workforce environment to assist employees in using their health care benefits. The care management programs are not meant to function as a general tool of support for an organization, but as a support for transition from one arena to the next.

Health care organizations that are involved in the transformation of care and care models must take this form of market response into consideration as they develop arrangements between and among providers. The concept of care management is actually a response to the failure and inadequacy of the organizations of the past (see Chapter 2) to impact any form of health care cost savings or quality improvement. This reflects an additional form of constraint for the system that needs to emerge.

If the past is a prologue for the future, the past programming is probably failing and the future programs have to be based upon a different framework. Both physicians and hospitals realize this. The resulting form, if it centers around health systems, will be structured on an employed physician base supplemented by a variety of contracted physician groups. For the health systems that do not have this form, marketplace forces will define how they coexist with payers and consumers.

Existing State, Near-Term Future State

Table 5.1 reflects the traditional, historical state of the marketplace and the near-term future state. Long term, who knows? Short term, a case can be made that several issues are in transition.

Table 5.1 Where Are We? Where Are We Headed?

	Traditional State	*Near-Term Future*
Physician networks	Inclusive	Selective
Health care services	Medically oriented	Consumer oriented
Medical care	Disease oriented	Health oriented
Care-focused planning	Individual	Population
Capital focus	Treatment technologies	Information technologies
Purchaser focus	Price/cost	Value

Final Note—What Is a Doula?

A doula is a person who assists a pregnant woman through childbirth and who has developed a relationship that is similar to the care manager that is described in the preceding paragraphs. The doula often accompanies the woman throughout the process and becomes a "pregnancy care navigator." The reference here is to challenge the reader to an understanding that these doulas in some areas of the country can become involved in unexpected ways to channel or steer choice of obstetricians, women's services, hospitals, etc. They are not generally credentialed and organized within any kind of a structure, but they can have the same type of impact that a care manager might have who is managing a large group of diabetics or asthmatics.

The point is that the systems that are emerging will articulate with systems that understand their needs and respect them. The health care contracting organization of the past did not need to understand concepts like care management and the existence of doulas. Those that are successful in the future will need to accommodate them along with many other forms of consumer channeling.

Summary Issues

- Not only are systems changing for the provision of care, but the purchasing models are changing on a profound level as well. The velocity of this change is unknown.
- Consumer channels for purchasing are changing with consequences that are difficult to predict. More information will soon be available to consumers who will be more often choosing with a direct financial stake in the choice.
- Web technologies are emerging that will have an additional effect upon choice. Like most emerging technology, this effect is impossible to predict.

Chapter 6

The Basic PHO (Joint Governance) or IPA (Independence)

The physician-hospital organization (PHO) is revisited here because it is a ubiquitous organization that is installed in many health care enterprises. Given the nature of bureaucracies, it is something that may not go away, even if it is dysfunctional or unable to achieve the goals that are necessary in a new marketplace of consumer choice and competitive insurance exchanges. Can the PHO transform itself into a functioning accountable care organization (ACO)? Probably not, unless it is structured in a fashion that will be able to effectively plan and react. This takes an organization that is focused on the needs of the marketplace and not the needs of its constituencies.

The PHO (and the corollary organization—the independent provider association (IPA)) is addressed here because it is probably something that is already in existence and which has an existing membership, infrastructure, and governance process. It may also have restrictions on its membership that restrain them from making determinations about moving their loyalties or membership to another organization. The idea and the basic premise of the IPA/PHO is not an impediment unless the organization itself is. Can the organization transform itself to address new challenges and new opportunities? The traditional medical staff cannot, by its very nature of being all-inclusive, become the contracting engine that will address newly emerging market demands from organized purchasers. Each IPA and PHO is a separate and distinct entity, and there may be some that can actually rise to the challenges of the modern contracting environment.

One way to find out is to simply ask the following questions. A series of no answers will indicate that the PHO/IPA is not a vehicle for change and transformation, but an impediment.

Do we have sufficient primary care practices with capacity capable of acquiring new patients in the near-term future that are dedicated to the organization and its members?

Can we contract on behalf of our membership using a "single signature" to bind all members?

Do we have sufficient management and core infrastructure to be able to communicate effectively internally and to implement programming across all components of our membership?

Do we have a governance process that can deal with membership challenges? That is, can we add doctors on a need basis and can we exclude doctors from contracting if they do not meet standards to which we have agreed?

These are pretty basic questions, but they should be at the core of the process to define the effectiveness and capabilities of an organization that can exist and thrive in the emerging marketplace. The corollary to the questions might be, "If we are not there yet, can we get there?" If not, it may be time for a new organization.

New organizations are sometimes spawned from traditional structures, but not if they have to carry the impediments and traditions that kept the previous organizations from being successful. If there is going to be reorganization under some new structure, it is necessary to figure out what to do with the old structure. In another section of the book, we address a relatively new form of hospital and physician collaboration—the contracted physician groups. We recognize that the traditional voluntary medical staff is a structure that will probably be left in place. They are in a form that has, over the years, been relegated to almost an honorary status in most hospitals, and while they do not generally have a structure that impedes contracting, they do not provide a basis of any kind for it.* With the medical staff and the contracted practices as links to the hospital, where does the PHO overlap, contribute, or compete?

As represented in Figure 6.1, the PHO takes over for the medical component and becomes the contracting arm for the providers. However, if the providers also

* One area in which the traditional medical staff may impede contracting is where a particular department can block or engage in behavior that limits access to medical staff credentials or departmental privileges. If the hospital finds itself in the position of having to go to the medical staff (or to a department within it) to get permission to add a doctor to the schedule in a GI lab or a cardiology procedural unit, then the medical staff is acting in a fashion that is in need of challenge. The medical staff should always address quality and performance matters but should never be in a position to restrict access to resources from otherwise qualified providers.

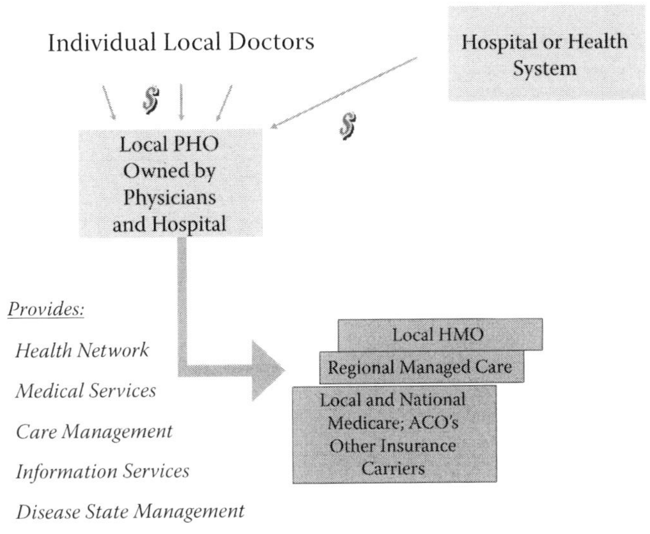

Figure 6.1 A PHO model that is ready for modern contracting.

contract independently, then the function of the PHO is limited to being just one additional provider in the marketplace.

It may be time to look at the organization and ask about its core goals and even address whether it should be expanded, reformatted, or abandoned. In Chapter 2, the basic building blocks of integration were outlined. Here are some of the guiding principles that an IPA/PHO probably espoused and which may be helpful to review with its leadership as this process of development proceeds.

- This organization was founded on the premise that it would use market coverage and scale as an advantage in contracting in order to achieve what a single physician or independent practice might not. Has it done that? Can it do that?
- New forms of payment are being discussed—pay for performance, value-based contracting, results-based payments, etc. Is the organization ready to take these on?
- New medical groups are forming and existing ones are expanding. Competitors are (or may be soon) contracting directly with individual doctors. Can we provide a competitive alternative?
- New technologies are emerging. Can the organization assist member practices in capital-intensive development processes that may include electronic medical records, information exchanges, consumer web marketing, etc.?

- National, state, and regional health systems are in transition. New initiatives at all levels require a higher level of intelligence for the physician than ever before. Does this group have the infrastructure to keep pace?
- Capital is often necessary for expansion, succession, business transformation, etc. Can the organization act on behalf of its members to capitalize the necessary projects?

Organizations have a tendency toward stagnation, and if there is a need for energizing an existing IPA or PHO, the idea should be to totally reengineer the organization starting with the basics and with a process that examines the mission statement, the membership, and the entire infrastructure. If any of these factors are not in alignment with each other, or not in conformance with the near-term needs of the competitive marketplace, then the best thing to do may be to form a new organization. One should reference the many ACOs around the country and see how many are being formed on traditional PHO structures—not many and maybe not any.*

The challenges inherent in the idea of an independent provider association, especially one that includes a hospital in some kind of collaborative role, is that there needs to be some kind of individual submission to the collective contracting effort. If the group is comprised of independent practices, they need to be willing (and able) to share core information and to transmit data on patients. They need to identify and foster relationships with specialists who can also share information openly. They need to be able to assist and support a robust governance model that reflects a combination of individual input and personal involvement as well as a shared commitment to a central effort of some kind.

Added to all of these factors is the issue of size. The group, if it is to be successful, will have to achieve a critical mass (sufficient numbers of doctors and practices) so that it can command a market position. In order to achieve the goals of integration (called for under almost all of the contracting forms that are now emerging), there will need to be collective information technology of some kind and a high level of commitment to not only sharing data but also the acceptance of common protocols.

---

* The Centers for Medicare and Medicaid Services (CMS) defines an ACO this way on its website: "groups of doctors, hospitals, and other health care providers, who come together voluntarily to give coordinated high quality care to their Medicare patients." It further states that "the goal of coordinated care is to ensure that patients, especially the chronically ill, get the right care at the right time, while avoiding unnecessary duplication of services and preventing medical errors." Few PHOs or IPAs are structured to achieve these goals. CMS, http://www.cms.gov/Medicare/Medicare-Fee-for-Service-Payment/ACO/index.html?redirect=/aco/.

Summary Issues

- Most hospitals and doctors are invested in the wrong type of an organization.
- Physicians and hospitals are slow to change their organizational structures, and most will suffer for this lack of flexibility and responsiveness.
- Those who are the first to adopt will have a marginal advantage over their competition.
- New competitors are emerging that not only will not follow the rules as they are presently understood, but also will be in a position to make new rules that the "old guard" will have to acknowledge and follow.

Chapter 7

The MSO (Services)

Any survey of hospital executives shows that they perceive that their institutions either are or will be attempting to develop some kind of formal relationship with select elements of the medical staff. As described elsewhere in this book, these efforts may take many forms, and the most effective are generally the most costly and politically risky. Many "social" approaches have been attempted that address some form of practice enhancement or the development of educational or informal management support services. Most hospitals are in an environment where there is already a reorganization of equity, which is really a euphemism for the purchase or capitalization of practices. Most hospital systems have already addressed the more straightforward and traditional approaches, like assistance with recruitment and coordination of promotional programming, and they are either ready for the next step or being forced to find one.

If there is any middle ground that spans many programs and areas of medical staff initiatives, it might be the management services organization (MSO). This is a structure that is one of the more flexible and functional approaches to bonding with physicians. The core component of an MSO is a defined array of services to doctors structured in a cooperative fashion. Often initially funded by the health care system, the MSO avoids fraud and abuse or inurement challenges* by developing a revenue base and a customer panel that manages the service mix. The MSO can build trust and a business relationship between a hospital and its physicians when

* These are all regulatory terms that are defined elsewhere in this book. They are useful to reference more than once since every physician-hospital organization should reference potential hazards in these areas and structure transactions and relationships with assistance from a competent attorney with health care regulatory experience.

the issues of governance and management are balanced between the expectations of the individual doctor and the needs of the health care system.

The advent of the electronic medical record (EMR), and the need for additional capital and the fact that this is a safe haven area for hospitals to advise and assist physicians, has been a boon to the MSO structure. The MSO can also be a transitional phase between the hospital assisting the practice and supporting the practice and then, eventually, incorporating the practice within the overall health care enterprise.

The MSO is also a model that appeals to doctors who want to be in some kind of a group but who do not want to actually incorporate together formally or develop a more concrete partnership. This structure allows doctors to form a sort of co-op, which can be the start of collaboration but along the lines that other independent businesses have formed in seeking noncompetitive cooperation. A business buying group is an example as is a farm grange or mill. The term that comes to mind when fiercely independent business entities get together to collaborate on some kind of common capital-intensive initiative is prairie communism. This is the example of two farms buying one tractor or thresher or the farmers in a community forming a grange.*

Most hospitals are in the throes of redefining their relationships with the marketplace, the consumer, and the distribution base in a free-for-all scramble to maintain market share at a time when the overall market is decreasing and the revenue per sale is being adjusted downward as well. Operational costs and capital needs continue unabated, and the options for alternative outpatient business development are met with competition from the very distributors and vendors the administrator must work with to achieve inpatient equilibrium. Adding to the unequal playing field created by collaborating with doctors on inpatient care while competing with them in the outpatient environment is the advantage that the privately capitalized entity has when competing with public and nonprofit health care institutions. Legally, and from the perspective of the public trust, the private entrepreneur can be much more flexible and responsive.

Doctors are witnessing both a real and an anticipated loss of actual spending power. Their practices have suffered from continued inflationary pressures, even in times of economic decline and minimal inflation in the general economy. This, coupled with the impact of a resource-based relative value scale (RBRVS), increasing emphasis on managed care, and an administration with a mandate to change health care delivery, has caused increasing numbers of physicians to seek alliances. These take the form of group practice development, physician-hospital

* A farm grange is a form of co-operative that is generally associated with a granary or with a common milling and processing plant of some kind. In Iowa and Nebraska, the farmers collaborate on any number of capital items and often share tractors and threshers. They meet at the "grange hall" to discuss how to allocate capital and assess costs for usage.

organizations (PHOs), independent provider associations (IPAs), consolidations, mergers, and acquisitions. Whatever the form, it is happening in every community.

The typical marketing orientation toward the physician by the hospital has been to assist and enhance the private practice, develop sales programs and product line initiatives, and even to assist in recruiting. Because of the issues inherent in regulatory requirements such as inurement and fraud and abuse, the options have to be more carefully constructed. Yet, this is occurring at a time when more is being demanded by the doctors because of the acute pressures that they perceive in the environment. Most hospital-oriented marketing efforts, however constructed, are inadequate when viewed from the physician perspective, especially if the doctor is in some kind of transitional stage in his or her practice (growth, start-up, slowdown, or anticipation of exit).

The Basic MSO Approach

The idea is to design a partnership with key physicians to develop an organization that functions as a business. This needs capital, an infrastructure, governance, and a ready market for its services. However, since the MSO almost always serves the practices that make up its governance structure and ownership, there is really no barrier to finding a market. The market research is pretty automatic, and the fulfillment of any delivery of goods and services is to a captive customer base. Market research—just ask the customers to give up their practice specifics, and the result is a base of services against which an operational department can be designed. Generally, the MSO is structured around key services that are essential to any physician practice. These include billing and collections and regulatory compliance matters. There is always a temptation to form a buying co-operative, and the group often meets for collaborative discussions on practice strategies and on contracting.*

The key to this sort of an initiative is the continued accommodation of physician autonomy without forcing the doctors into something that is perceived as hospital ownership. If physician assets are owned, it is by the co-operative. Independence is maintained, or at least the semblance of independence is maintained since co-op ownership requires a different level of respect and coordination among the physicians. Like any good business, this one should operate from a written plan with realistic expectations and a defined governance structure. If the business plan reflects a "no dividend" situation or one where the customer list is the same as the group

* This is an area where there should be a cautionary note about antitrust and fraud and abuse. Physician groups that are in an unconsolidated association (not under a single corporate structure and tax identification number) cannot collaborate on prices for their services or discuss any form of refusing service to a particular contracting group or collection of patients. This is one of the limitations of this structure. They can purchase together and contract together for services.

of owners, then the MSO is defined as a mutual or a member-owned entity, but if there is residual (profit) to be shared with a specific class of owners without referencing the customer base, then the MSO is a standard business, and it should follow all of the rules, express and implied, that would define what typical business owners might do without referencing the customer base except in a marketing sense.

The services that are key to an MSO, initially, usually include overall management and consultative practice reviews, billing and collection, equipment and personnel pooling, risk management, recruiting, etc. The key is to allow the doctors to be involved in an advisory policy-making capacity to prioritize efforts and to pick services that will have universal appeal, applications that are apolitical, and immediate payback. Eventually (and hopefully), the MSO can assist in preparing practices for managed care coordinated contracting, equity transition (sale or retirement), mergers, and acquisitions. The key is to get a stable group of practitioners involved in a collaborative process that can allow them to participate with the hospital in developing initiatives and services from the traditional co-op model. That is, if there are savings or reductions in service cost, the group shares in them through a dividend or a reduction in fees after the health system has recovered its initial investment.

The MSO is a transitional entity. Most health care futurists believe the eventual model will be a community-based health care system with providers and consumers involved in caregiving and "care paying" considerations. Group practices, PHOs, and preferred provider organizations (PPOs) are all steps in the learning curve for most communities. The MSO allows a hospital and a group of supportive physicians a chance to practice at the art of collaborative planning and product delivery in a virtually threat-free fashion while they ponder the next step. Providers who have developed strong relationships through less formal, albeit effective, means will be considering different structures as the health care system is regenerated in the idea of a managed competition model. For most of the physicians who did not fare well under competition and who abhor managed care, the thought that the next phase of the delivery system will combine these aspects will be enough to send them to the nearest administrator seeking shelter of some kind. Sales and liaison programs simply will not suffice.

MSO Development

The steps to create an MSO are rather straightforward. However, while they are easily described, the simplicity of the structure can be deceiving. This type of project takes a great deal of hard work, planning, and communication. It should be developed by experienced teams who are comfortable (and effective) in implementing successful physician practice management services.

- The medical staff development plan must be reviewed to see that it is up to date and functional. It is important to construct MSO programs that complement rather than compete with other efforts.
- The medical staff planning function must be related to a financial payback or cost-benefit analysis. Expenditures are going to be required, and the implication is that there must also be a payback for any new initiative that is going to sustain the health care system's support in these trying and competitive times.
- An assessment of the services available to doctors in the community, both from the health care system and from the marketplace, must be made. Doctors know what is already out there, and we must likewise be aware before we take them a program (if we are to have any credibility).
- A short list of likely customers (candidates for both service provision and board participation) must be developed. These must be successful players, not candidates for rescue missions. The practitioner must be one whose practice is relatively stable and one that contributes to the goals of the institution.
- Develop a listing of resources and services that the MSO might provide, hopefully those that the health system can launch with an efficient and effective start-up. Remember, these have to be universal, and they must have a financial impact on the practice. They should be well defined (billing, collection, personnel) rather than generic (education, coordination, consulting).
- Develop a *pro forma* that capitalizes the business and initiates the core services at a cost recapture level. The board of consumer-doctors will keep the process honest.
- Initial meetings can be used to prioritize activities, address membership or customer issues, plan for intermediate and longer-range services, fine-tune governance, and qualify additional activities. The goal is to allow the initial group to succeed and build a base of services that can attract other practitioners through an obviously successful track record.

An MSO isn't the only answer, but it is an important transitional structure that can be used effectively in developing medical staff relationships beyond the "flirting and dating" stages. While many of us know, or think we know, where the game is going (i.e., group practices and the community-coordinated models), few can figure out how to get there. This stage offers one step that will help to build interrelationships between providers and at the same time put potential competitors into a collaborative model that can be used to develop a business relationship.

Functional Operations

The MSO would employ all the nonprofessional staff for all physician practices. This would include job titles such as receptionist, medical assistant, biller, secretary, office manager, nurse (LPN or RN), surgery scheduler, precertification specialist, radiology technologist, etc. There would be established salary ranges, job descriptions, and benefit plans for each position that would be consistent from practice to practice.

The MSO would own all the tangible assets—buildings, equipment, furniture, etc. The MSO would pay all the bills and provide all services to the practices, including accounting, legal, payroll, trash pickup, purchasing, etc. Anything that the practice needs, the MSO would provide. The hope would be that some economies of scale would exist that would save money over the entire spectrum of practices managed.

The MSO would provide IT support in the way of Internet access, e-mail, server support, backup, security, hardware installation and maintenance, software training, electronic medical records software, and all practice management software. This idea of an MSO providing the computers and software is attractive to a hospital that is trying to consolidate information systems. It means that the hospital (or the MSO) can dictate the platform on which the doctors congregate, and that means that there is a much better chance that the final data (patient information) will have some consistency and that the systems will interact for the purposes of registration, file sharing, and data interchanges.*

Each "practice" could be a division within the MSO (for data reporting and management purposes). Standardized profit and loss (P&L) and accounts receivable reports would be prepared for each practice as well as in total for the MSO on a monthly basis. There would be one tax return for the MSO and one for each professional corporation remaining in place.

The executive director would be responsible overall for the management of all practices and would act as liaison with his or her counterpart at the hospital. All other MSO staff would report to him or her. The physicians would be hired through one or a combination of professional corporations, which would allow them the flexibility to be participating or nonparticipating with key health care insurance plans. They would have a different benefit structure from the MSO employees and, over time, a compensation methodology that, at its core, addresses each provider in a similar manner in terms of compensation. The goal is to narrow the variability of functions throughout the various professional corporations and to arrive at a point where there are only two or three corporations to deal with in terms of providers. Key considerations in determining how many corporations are needed and what type(s) of corporations they should be could include P&L potential, similarity of operations, and so forth.

* The OIG advisory opinion published in December 2012 gave hospitals the green light to support physician practices in their quest for electronic health record (EHR)/EMR interoperability, and the MSO is a convenient platform on which to do just that. OIG Advisory Opinion 12-20, https://oig.hhs.gov/fraud/docs/advisoryopinions/2012/AdvOpn12-20.pdf.

Financial Operations

The MSO would charge a management fee to each practice for which it provides services. The fee could be a percent of revenue (except in states where this is not allowed by statute).* One way to calculate this would be to have the global fee approximate average nonphysician overhead in the practice historically or base it on national benchmarks (the Medical Group Management Association (MGMA) might be one such source). Another method would be to charge a fixed fee based on the market in addition to the actual costs of all services, goods, and staff provided.

The MSO would provide financial statements for each division managed on a monthly basis, which would include, but not be limited to, the following: income and expense statement, monthly accounts receivable (AR) reports to include at least an aged AR by payer class, productivity reports by provider and by financial class, total charges, payments and adjustments by financial class, etc. The idea is to provide useful periodic information in order to keep the physicians involved and engaged in the financial operations of the practice.

Advances made to practices would be recorded and repaid. Excess profits, above and beyond the management fees and compensation to physicians could, in theory, be used to repay advances made by the hospital, or shared between the MSO and the physician owners of the corporation.

Goals of the MSO/Vendor Group

These are pretty simple, but they bear listing and referring to in the process of "selling" this concept to the proposed participants. Each stakeholder that looks at an MSO sees a different potential for this arrangement. Actually, the pure co-op definition is the best. There is a scope and a purpose to this type of an organization that is better narrow than broad. The broader the scope, the more difficult it will be to manage the MSO, especially with both hospital and physician representatives involved in the governance process.

Try a simple, two-pronged set of objectives and then assess the MSO process and progress against each. This will force clarity in the governance of the organization, and staff will know their roles and responsibilities.

- To provide operating efficiencies for the group that ultimately stabilize/reduce overhead

* Percentage billing arrangements and percentage management arrangements are frowned upon in some states since they are perceived as the "corporate" practice of medicine. In these cases, a flat fee is constructed that is reassessed on a periodic basis. Of course, competent legal counsel familiar with the regulations in the state in which the program is being developed will have the final word on contract compliance with regulatory issues of this nature.

- To support and enhance growth of the physician organization including its market share

Operational Responsibilities of the MSO/Vendor Group

1. Hire, evaluate, promote, and discharge all employees. This would mean that all present employees of the physician group would become employees of the MSO/vendor entity. Hopefully, salaries and benefits would remain at their historic levels. There is no intent to change this structure to be in line, or competitive, with the sponsoring hospital/system employee salaries and benefits. However, all responsibility for personnel decisions would be under the sphere of the MSO, and individual employees would no longer be accountable directly to the group or its physicians independently. Input from physicians would be required in order to manage staff effectively, efficiently, and fairly.
2. Negotiate all contracts with other subcontractors. This would include the purchase of all equipment, supplies, and services. Services include those of the medical specialists.
3. Negotiate contracts for managed care, etc. Jointly, with the physician corporate negotiators, contracts for managed care such as IPA, PPO, HPO, etc., would be handled by the MSO/vendor group.
4. Manage the day-to-day operations of all facilities and services provided under the umbrella of the physician group.
5. Provide for strategic planning, implementation, and recruitment of physicians to expand the services provided by the physicians and thereby expand market share in the area.

What Does the MSO Not Do?

There are some limitations and these are purposeful. The MSO does not have a professional billing number, so the practice(s) must maintain individual billing status and perform all of the functions associated with coding and submittal of claims. Each practice has its own tax identification number and files an individual tax return. Most important, the practice manages its physician complement and defines how income is distributed. The practice has final say over its managed care contracting, pricing, and financial relationships with its customers. This means that it retains control over write-offs and collections policies.

Summary Issues

- MSOs are in vogue right now since they represent a transitional state between pure independence and some kind of co-joined equity (or outright practice sale).
- Some features of the MSO are especially attractive to hospitals since they are a buffer between the hospital and the doctors, and they keep practices at arm's length.
- Challenges remain because of the inability of the MSO to really contract on behalf of a unified provider group. The MSO can provide the infrastructure for contracting but not the corporate platform.
- MSOs are simple in concept but complex to execute. Challenges relate to bookkeeping and governance.

Chapter 8

Co-Management Programs (Partnership)

It is an attractive thought. The hospital and the physicians might be able to manage some component of health care together and reduce the tension that is created by their individual roles in the process. This is the background objective of a co-management agreement. These are collaborative arrangements where a variety of vendors enter into an agreement to identify a specific product line or collection of services. The examples include orthopedics, cardiology and open heart surgery, vascular, obstetrics and gynecology, and oncology. In each case there are a variety of providers and caregivers and a specific type of health care delivery involved.

This is population management for a specific segment of the population that has been defined by their disease or condition rather than their payment category or demographic. It assumes that everyone and anyone that walks through a hospital portal or any kind of entry point, for that matter, will be managed by a team that has the broad charge of simply doing a great job for the patients in their particular discipline. As a corollary, the hospital and the providers who share the responsibility also share the income and the upsides and downsides related to the patient population being managed.

The co-management model theoretically brings every aspect of care under a committee that is comprised of the doctors who provide and prescribe the care and the hospital that typically has the capital involved in the facility and technical component of the process. This takes the medical staff concept with all of its political implications out of the picture* and replaces it with a group governance that includes those doctors who want to be much more involved in the oversight of the processes that impact their patients. This is not done without including them also in the revenue streams of the processes managed. The success or failure of the entire venture is projected on one balance sheet and income and expense statement. If the enterprise does well, then everyone does well. The converse case is also true.

Getting There Is (More Than) Half the Battle

This is a structure where one must ask how to get from point A to point B. Once the idea of a co-management structure is agreed upon, the idea of how to reorganize the facility component with the therapeutic and diagnostic services in some kind of recognizable unit that can submit to a governance change is easier said than done. Sometimes, it really cannot be done. Add the complexity of the coordination or subordination of a private practice and the way in which the practice operates on top of this to create some kind of seamless (or at least barrier-free) organization, and the challenges mount. However, the result can generally be easily agreed upon, and the issues that must be overcome can always be identified. This may be the time to reflect on the Kettering adage that a problem that has been defined is more than half solved.† This is an area where the planning process has to precede the implementation; otherwise, since there is not any one best co-management structure and no way to really anticipate how the process between a hospital and physicians might design such a thing, there is a danger that the result might actually be new, but not necessarily "new and improved."

The entire process rests on a description of where everyone agrees that the co-management process is headed. This is where operational and project planning must be employed, not just some kind of general idea about a direction or a philosophy. This is where an independent planner or some kind of an intermediary with some objectivity may be important. Where we are is often confused with where we want to be. The issue is to define a complete reorganization of the programming and make sure that the existing structures are not barriers to achieving the end result. An example for orthopedics is offered as a guide to discussion. This is a

* Actually, there is still a medical staff structure, but the co-management organization is superimposed on top of it so that the actual credentialing, quality assurance, and professional interrelationships are more precisely managed and more specifically outlined.

† Charles Kettering was an engineer and inventor with almost 200 patents to his credit. Many of the things that comprise a modern automobile were originally designed by Kettering. He is credited with many observations and axioms that transcend engineering and are useful when one thinks about general problem solving. This is one of his most often quoted adages, and it is referenced here because a health care organization moving quickly will sometimes simply begin the journey to a solution when the actual issues have not yet been defined. Design should follow definition.

simple example that could be implemented in a structure in which there is a series of transactions that lead to a practice purchase, or it could be externalized to a more complex process that includes a full joint venture on an independent ownership structure for an ASC* and a resulting management services organization (MSO), jointly owned by a hospital and the doctors, which would manage the ASC, the orthopedic practices, and all of the hospital processes generally connected with bone and joint disease processes.

An Orthopedic Co-Management Model

There will be an oversight committee comprised of the orthopedic specialists, hospital administrative staff, and primary care physicians who will directly manage all functions related to the specialty of orthopedics (musculoskeletal injuries, bone and joint diseases, orthopedics, rehabilitation, bone mass preservation and restoration, related trauma, and durable medical equipment), which will encompass outpatient functions, the medical specialties involved in orthopedics, community-based programs, inpatient resources, surgery and imaging functions, etc. Essentially, anything related to the processing of a patient relative to musculoskeletal issues will report to this oversight group.

Figure 8.1 is a schematic of the structure of the resulting organization. Accreditation and credentialing requirements related to the hospital board oversight functions will be preserved and acknowledged by this group, and they will take full responsibility for maintaining all medical staff duties and quality assurance processes that are associated with the program. The hospital functions and the outpatient and community-based functions will all be related through one set of registration criteria, and the involvement of all of the factors of contracting with external managed care groups will also be coordinated to assure that there is a program that is fully engaged in serving all of the community health care needs as they may relate to the functions controlled by this co-management team.

As displayed above, this is a functional management structure that has lines and boxes. It ignores the fact that there has to be a general agreement on how each component is going to be managed and contracted. One would assume that most stakeholders are in the governance process someplace, or that they are a subcontractor to the co-management organization.

If one can define what is "in," then it is easy to define what is not and to develop a scope and purpose for what we are calling here, for lack of a better term, the oversight committee.

---

* ASC is the acronym commonly applied to a freestanding ambulatory surgery center.

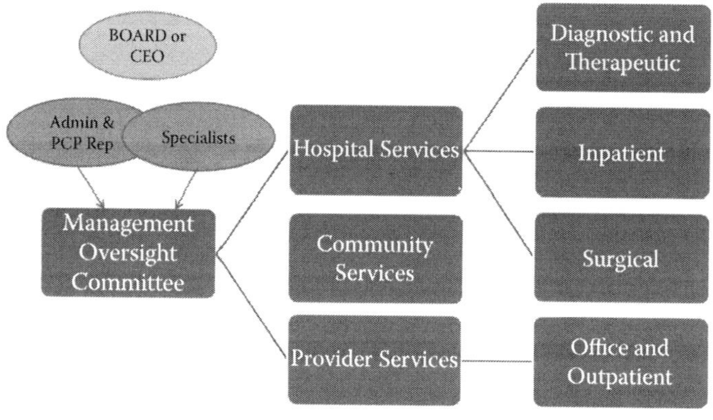

Figure 8.1 A co-management model that encompasses hospital services.

This group will, in conjunction with staff support from the various entities incorporated within the program, do the following:

- Address any budget issue related to investment in orthopedic programming
- Manage the overall orthopedic patient experience for all components that are involved in bone and joint programming
- Incorporate all stakeholders associated with orthopedics into one coordinated function that is presented to the community as a unified bone and joint program
- Develop a plan that is oriented to assure continued community availability of orthopedics and orthopedic services
- Coordinate ancillaries to assure that they can be managed through emerging payment methodologies
- Align the product line organization and management functions to assure that the goals of all the parties are the same or similar, or at least not internally competitive

If the institution and the physicians have a unified vision, it seems simple that the program planning and implementation would be smooth, but this is where the near-term and long-term plans must include a factor that relates to the distribution of any margin and define how this will be incorporated within the physician distribution program. This is more easily done if the income functions are internally planned and have some type of parity between the physicians. If the incomes of the doctors remain under the control of their private practice agreements and largely oriented to fee-for-service volume and revenue results, the oversight committee must be sensitive to working with that structure to assure that there are real cost savings and quality metrics that can be delivered in the community or to those who would want to contract with the co-management group.

A key factor in the co-management structure is the issue of being committed to joint contracting. This is formalized by having many (all) of the contracting functions become subject to a restrictive covenant to which each party subscribes. This means that the practices and the doctors can only function and contract through the enterprise, but it also means that any development or recruitment that the hospital might elect is also done through this partnership. Both parties become linked in a state of interdependence that produces the benefits of coordination, but the limitations of shared governance and mutual decision making.

Special mention should be made about the parallel hospital department and medical staff section that comprises the co-management physician team. In this case, that might be the orthopedic specialists and physiatrists. They are contiguous with the group of doctors "managed" through the co-management model, so the standards should be complementary but not necessarily the same since doctors other than those on the medical staff may be part of a co-management venture. The management resources and committee structures can be the same, or overlap, but the membership of the hospital medical staff may not need to be exactly congruous with every part of the product line. The reason that orthopedics was chosen as an example is because there may be a reason to include doctors of chiropractic and podiatrists and physical therapists in the programming.

The co-managed process requires some basic pieces, and the rest is up to the planning process. It certainly requires both a hospital and a group of doctors. It also has to have a charter and a basic plan that describes where it is going. There should be some kind of exclusive dealing* defined. A unified budget process and a budget with capital planning are imperative. If a group governs itself but has no budgeting process, it is not managing anything except protocols and policies. The budget implies that this group will have some contracting capabilities, and that the group will also oversee hiring and job determinations for the staff involved in the project.

If there are barriers to incorporating a management or oversight committee function within the hospital structure, it can be used as an advisory function and its members can be empowered on all of the parallel committees that have hospital stature and related powers. When the co-management session opens for business, the medical staff secretary can be present to offer some of the issues related to formal medical staff committee functions, and the meetings can be held in the same space and overlap since the orthopedic surgeons that comprise the stakeholders of the co-management program are also the ones who are probably the majority in any hospital committee. For the purposes of HR and staff oversight, the requirement

---

* This was described earlier in this chapter in the form of a mutual restrictive covenant.

of involvement by a doctor is routine in conducting a 360° personnel evaluation,* and this can be channeled to the co-management team to appoint someone to participate.

The real challenge in all of this is determining how the doctors will be compensated. There should be some basic level of compensation that is market driven. The physicians will have to understand that they are working for a scale of some kind, and that the scale for which they are working is fair market value. The bonus dollars have to be driven by the success factors agreed upon for the product line. This is what aligns the goals and rewards of the hospital and the physician group, and it is the one key item that drives the collaborative decision making throughout the process. Therefore, a bookkeeping and benchmarking system has to be created that can be shared among partners, physicians, and their hospital administration partners. This has to be understandable and directly related to the effort that is expended within the co-management process. It also has to reflect some of the important impact areas that are under the direct control of the doctors.

This will be a recurrent theme under integrated models that incorporate the physician. Their bonus has to be linked to the success of the organization, and its goals and the benchmarks have to be understandable and must reflect factors that the doctor can actually manage. If the doctor had a previous employment life that was dictated by pure volume and this will change, what will actually change if the only factor is a new way to count volume? Subsequent chapters will share one approach to this that can be modified to suit any number of situations, but what is described on these pages is a mechanical process. The real problem is to relate the mechanics to the situational planning and overall process of operational delivery of health care.

Development Process

Simple steps in this process mask a complex structure and an even more complex result. However, the first steps involve concept and buy-in. The hospital and its various stakeholders have to understand the co-management idea and its implications. This means that the various areas that are going to be involved have to agree to the idea and submit in some way to being managed in a different way. In the case of orthopedics, our example, this will mean the involvement of the inpatient floor (nursing administration), imaging (the radiologists), access points (the ED and employed primary care, especially in urgent care sites), and therapy units (physical

* The idea of a 360° evaluation is not new, but it may be to some health care organizations. The concept is that a person's annual or periodic review is done by many people—supervisor, subordinates, coworkers, and customers. The results are then organized into one cohesive evaluation tool that is the final determinant for any action by the supervisor or executive in charge.

therapy and physiatrists). This is more than just a task force or a committee; it is the establishment of an alternate form of governance and oversight.

Doctors also have to have some level of buy-in along with their staff and advisors. A broad process of information delivery is necessary to assure that the co-management idea is delivered among any of the key parts of the delivery team, especially where there later might be some ability to hamper development through active or passive resistance. Here, it may be desirable to involve the doctors' legal counsel and tax counsel at an early stage to make sure that they understand the process and the desired outcomes. Otherwise, their questions and concerns may unravel the project during the contract development phase.

Common legal instruments necessary at this stage include a mutual nondisclosure agreement (NDA) and a memorandum of understanding (MOU) or a letter of intent (LOI). Some legal teams will resist the development of any sort of interim document that is not something with legal clout, but this process is complex enough that it needs interim documentation of everyone's intent and commitment. The NDA might also include a commitment to a timeline as well as a commitment to "exclusive dealing." The timeline is an obvious attempt to keep the planning and development group on track, but it also serves the purpose to create a little bit of friction for each party to move decision making along in a purposeful fashion. If there are legs in development, market conditions can change and intent can wane. Budgets and projections need to be recast, and other development activities might be delayed. Start to finish, any project that exceeds a 6- to 10-month time period is one that is in danger of having key elements of the deal or arrangement come under scrutiny two or three times by one party or another with the resulting risk that the arrangement will fold.

The idea of exclusive dealing holds both parties to the development of the product line only through the efforts of the team committed to the co-management project. This seems pretty obvious for the physician group as a criterion since it commits them to dealing with the hospital exclusively, and it takes them "out of the market" for other, sometimes competitive, opportunities. However, it does have implications for the hospital as well. The hospital cannot recruit another doctor of the same discipline or one that is closely aligned or related while the process is underway. The hospital cannot enter into a contract that is organized to service the orthopedic product or service line while the co-management project is being developed. It cannot replace orthopedic-related equipment or enter into an arrangement that would significantly alter physical medicine. This impacts a lot of other physician groups and activities in any number of hospital departments. For example, the development of a bone densitometry program to address osteoporosis may have any number of doctors and disciplines involved, but it would be delayed pending the organization of the co-management orthopedic project if a strong exclusive dealing arrangement was in place and honored by the hospital.

In order to contain some of the indecision (and anxiety), it is often helpful to initiate a long-term planning process that runs contiguous to the operational development process. This requires the team to agree upon an overall vision and some longer-term goals, and it may provide a channel for some of the other stakeholder groups to become involved without tying up the transactions that are being considered to bring the co-management program from an unformed idea to implementation. This will also tie the process to the hospital's overall plans and, especially if it is a nonprofit institution,* to the community service plan that aligns the institution with its local base. This will be a factor that will also assist consultants who might be involved with developing fair market value (FMV) opinions on some of the components of the program as the process moves from planning to transactions.

If all of the orthopedic physicians are going to be involved in a process that incorporates their practice in some way and which allows funds associated with the hospital to flow through some sort of predefined path, the team will be considering a series of contracts or outright purchase of the practices. Also, the services to patients within the practices themselves will be part of the overall product line profile and integrated with some precision requiring an operational oversight of the practice by the co-management group. In essence, if the practices are not purchased, the contracting will be almost as tight as if they were, and the steps to contract or cement the relationship through a purchase are pretty similar.

Following the execution of the NDA and the establishment of the overall goals and objectives of the program, there must be some level of due diligence of the practice and the related hospital programs. An overall schematic has to be developed that describes the baseline financials, and especially the process measures that are integral to the success of the project. The simplest measure, of course, is patients enrolled or patients served. However, the group should be focusing in the near term on all of the aspects of financial performance and on every aspect that defines patient care and consumer satisfaction. More patients served is but one measure, but it is one that might be simply the result of changes in demographics that have nothing to do with any component of the project itself.

One must constantly reflect on the fact that this type of a program is not typical for either the doctors or the hospital, and that some of the other related groups may be actually threatened by the new management imperative. In the recent past

* Not every hospital is nonprofit, and the author recognizes that distinction. However, most are, and the distinction in contracting and engaging physicians is slight. A nonprofit enterprise must have almost all of its contractual relationships with private parties within parameters that are based on fair market value in order to assure that IRS rules related to inurement are met. A for-profit organization does not have this standard for contracts and employment, but it must still heed all other regulatory standards that relate to fraud and abuse and Stark sanctions. This book does not pretend to give legal advice except to recommend that the reader who is unfamiliar with these terms will find them generally described in other chapters, but each is being continuously defined by case law and opinions, and any transaction between a hospital and its physicians should be reviewed by legal counsel who is experienced in health care.

between the principals, there was not any kind of overall stated agreement by either party on what direction orthopedic services should take in the local area, and the physicians operated on a pure fee-for-service budget. The hospital managed on a cost control basis, and there was little need for any kind of agreement over the values that each party assigned to resources or physician compensation. The new environment changes all of these definitions and exposes physician compensation to review and hospital overhead loading to inspection as well.

Whatever the form, there will be a number of contracting events, resulting in some kind of physician contract and pay scale being determined jointly. These agreements have to be developed along with the standards on which scale and bonuses will be paid. The following is a listing of terms that might be considered.

- Time dedicated to clinic activities
- Time dedicated to teaching efforts
- Time related to administrative processes
- Patients served, through process measures
- Physician adherence to established protocols and treatment algorithms
- Procedures and patients measured by work relative value units (WRVUs)
- Physician relative utilization of resources
- Patient satisfaction
- Physician 360° evaluation
- Citizenship issues

This is an area where we can see that the determination of quality is not directly addressed, but there are many aspects of what might contribute to overall quality incorporated within the standards for contracting. Whatever form the co-management structure takes, the idea of overall patient satisfaction and adherence to protocols suggests something like quality. This is a feature that will be repeated in any number of models, and it is the basis on which true integration is based.

The co-management structure has to exist within regulatory guidelines, but it also has to recognize that there is an established medical staff structure with credentialing, call requirements, teaching requirements, departments, meetings, etc. This can be easily incorporated within the co-management structure with some careful planning and secretarial support. The same meetings that are associated with the operational oversight of the co-management program can be used for medical department meetings and for quality assurance (QA) sessions. There simply needs to be a format agreed upon that allows the groups to overlap and for the appropriate secretaries from a variety of hospital process areas to attend and to take the necessary minutes for whatever format is necessary to maintain accreditation.

The other considerations relate to other programmatic initiatives that are embedded within the institution. In the case of orthopedics, there may already be programs that are organized around the specialty. These might include a back pain program, a special unit that does spine surgery, sports medicine, performance medicine, a bone preservation program, etc. Also, orthopedics might be directly involved in many other program initiatives. Pain and occupational medicine come to mind. Each has its own special identity and protocol set and operational structure. If one adds a co-management process, it has to be done with some care to carefully coordinate resources so that there is no internal competition that might offset any of the program advantages. Other considerations include the impact on medical teaching programs, research, staff education, call structures, department coverage, hospitalists, etc. In each case, there will be some kind of challenge that relates to articulation of a new management structure in a traditional hospital environment.

Summary Issues

- Co-management is a highly regarded form of integration that preserves some aspects of private practice and hospital autonomy but which defines collaboration around a particular product line. It is simple to discuss, hard to implement.
- Co-management addresses some problems but raises many challenges that might be underlying in hospital programs and undiscovered until the co-management process is engaged. These include questions about physician compensation for administrative and call functions and control issues over departments that have been traditionally managed by the hospital.
- Co-management often includes consolidation of services from the private practice with the hospital. An example might be the reorganization of imaging to combine the hospital unit with any others that have been provided through the private practice.
- Co-management efforts can raise political questions and turf issues. These can occur when traditional medical staff relationships and management structures are changed either purposely or accidentally, challenging other disciplines. Examples might include the management of patients in therapy units or in intensive care environments.

Chapter 9

Contracts and Subcontracts (Managing Relationships)

Physician-hospital organizations (PHOs), independent provider associations (IPAs), management services organization (MSOs), and co-management analyses will bring one to the question about simply just contracting for physician services. This is typical for hospital-based and dependent specialty groups like radiologists and pathologists. More recently, the emergency department (ED) physicians and hospitalists have been contracted to cover their respective areas of responsibility. There are also some other groups that might naturally be thought of as being best organized through contracting rather than by some other type of organization. These include intensivists, those doctors who cover the intensive care units, and in some isolated cases, proceduralists.

The idea of contracting to establish a specific medical staff component is not new, but doing the contracts to fulfill the needs of an integrated system is very new. The old style is pretty simple—trade coverage for an exclusive contract. The newer style calls for a scope of work definition that can challenge hospitals and doctors alike. Figure 9.1 offers a comparison.

Moving from one type of relationship to the next can be a challenge since the contracts of the professional corporation and the arrangements between and among the doctors may be a barrier to agreeing with a hospital- or market-mandated change or enhancement of some kind. For example, if the hospital requires the group to now achieve full participation in a local managed care plan that they

Contract Issue	Traditional	Modern
Length of Term	Longer with automatic renewals	Shorter, with no automatic renewal
Coverage	Implied	Defined
Service Measures	Assumed	Specified
Call/Call Compensation	Implied, included	Defined, negotiated
Billing Standards	Self-determined	Defined, consistent with hospital
Compliance	Self-administered	System-administered

Figure 9.1 Performance standards are emerging.

have not previously accepted, it may require the doctors to all be credentialed in that insurance product. However, if the doctors have constructed their group with some physicians who might not be eligible to be part of that insurance plan, the hospital contract cannot be fulfilled.

Compliance is another matter that is a challenge. If the hospital and the health system wish to contract for services on the basis of a nontraditional arrangement (not fee for service based), then the doctors have to be able to coordinate their fee schedules with that of the hospital in some fashion. If there is internal coding compliance and fair market value determinations that need to be demonstrated in the master contract, these requirements will flow through to the subcontractor, and they, the doctors, may not be structured or prepared to comply. The uncertain future demands that an organization be able to move quickly and decisively. Hospital-based specialty groups have to be contracted in a fashion that complements and supports this need.

Generally speaking, the process of contracting with hospital-based groups is one that is in need of redefinition and revision. These groups are generally in place for a very long time, and if that continued service is based upon merit and cost-effectiveness, then the continuing relationship makes sense. Most of the time the long-term relationship, at least with radiologists and anesthesiologists and pathologists, is simply the maintenance of the status quo. Hospital boards and their administrators should be reviewing these contracts and testing them against the market on a periodic basis, which means every 3 to 5 years. The test of a good contractual relationship is whether it meets the current needs of both parties and whether the contract terms are common for the type of service defined by the contract. The major mistakes that boards make is to assume that the services have to be in a contract form, and that the group and doctors presently providing the services are irreplaceable. Interestingly, these are the same assumptive errors made by the contracting group.

Rather than try to tell the reader what might be done and how to do it, the remainder of this chapter contains some examples that can be used as a guide in contracting with medical service providers. If one were to develop a policy for contracting, and many hospitals have done so, it would clearly state a duration for each type of contract and some general parameters for reaching a set of terms. These would include the specification of call coverage, the credentialing level of the doctors, and the way that the doctors and their organization will articulate. Hopefully, the contracting process will be moderated by a third party (not the manager directly involved in the department), and the contract scope will define the involvement of the group within the overall fabric of the hospital strategic planning and contracting process.

Example: A Hospital-Based Physician Arrangement (Hospitalists)*

Hospitalists are now a coverage asset within a health care institution that formerly was assumed to be simply part of the service profile that was provided through the general medical staff. Traditionally, doctors covered their own patients for admission and discharge processes and "rounded" on them, managing their care while during the inpatient process. The crisis in medical manpower and the changing demands for more standardized and predictable coverage patterns gave rise to a new form of physician—the hospitalist. This is loosely defined as a doctor or a provider that is dedicated to care within the confines of the hospital itself and who provides care for a class, or classes, of patients that are defined by contract and not by the fact that they are from the doctor's own independent practice. Presently, it is reported that there are over 30,000 practicing hospitalists and growing.†

However, hospitalist groups come from many sources, and the issue of definition of the source of the doctors is a determining factor in the general approach that might be taken in contracting with the hospitalist team (or group or corporation). These are the various sources from which the health care system might draw for hospital inpatient support.

- Practices native to the health care environment who have reorganized themselves into a hospitalist team for the purposes of the provision of contracted services
- A corporation that provides hospitalists as a unique and complete service

---

* Examples of this nature can be found and downloaded at www.medicalstaffintegration.org.

† Victoria Stagg Elliot, The Evolution of the Hospitalist, AMANEWS.com, September 3, 2012, http://www.amednews.com/article/20120903/business/309039970/4/. Ms. Stagg was quoting a statistic reported by the Society of Hospital Medicine.

Obviously, there are many relationship issues and political trip wires faced by a health care system that contracts with a group defined from within the existing medical staff. Rules relating to the medical staff will conflict and overlap with the contract points that are necessary to define the hospital coverage needs, and there is the overlap of the physician covering for his or her own patients while covering for the general hospital population. There is also the issue of contracting and how the contracts can be fairly structured when all, or part, of the doctors have ties with medical practices that are on the voluntary medical staff.

Political issues aside, the process for contracting and for defining coverage is rather straightforward. Also, there is the emergence of a variety of national standard setting organizations, although relative to other specialties, the discipline of the physician as a "hospitalist specialist" is still probably emerging. One organization that might take issue with this statement is the Society of Hospital Medicine,* which is a national group that generally reflects the industry trends and lobbies on behalf of hospitalists. Without commenting on the status of the discipline or its long-term position in the fabric of the integrated system, there are some basic contract processes that can be applied.

Hospitalist Group Contract Points/Coverage Terms

1. Define the time coverage parameters. What hours will the hospitalist team cover? Full 24/7/365? Nights and weekends only?
2. Define the coverage service. For what groups of patients will the hospitalist provide service? All admitted patients? Only those patients who have doctors whose practices elect hospital coverage? Ad hoc coverage—as needed, when needed? Certain classes of patients that are categorized by payer category? Certain classes of patients that are defined by disease state categories?
3. Define the group makeup and composition. Are the doctors all dedicated hospitalists or are they from the medical staff? Are the doctors a homogeneous group of specialists or have they a variety of backgrounds and specialties? Are mid-level providers allowed to make up part of the coverage team?
4. Define the hospitalist role in the care of the patient. What can hospitalists do and when can they do it? Are they to admit the patient and follow him or her while in the hospital for his or her entire span of admission? Do they admit the patient, write initial orders, and transition the patient to his or her own primary care or specialist physician? Do they discharge the patient?

* The Society of Hospital Medicine was formed in 2003. It was formerly known as the National Association of Inpatient Physicians. Its membership is reported at over 10,000 and growing. It is comprised of both physicians and mid-level providers, and it is the main membership, publishing, and advocacy representative of the hospitalist industry. http://www.hospitalmedicine.org/.

5. Define the span of control. Does the hospitalist have final say in ordering tests and diagnostic procedures? Can the hospitalist intervene in care and define a course of action? How much collaboration is required (desired or dictated)?
6. Define other support functions. Does the hospitalist support the intensive care units? Does the hospitalist act as a peak loading support team member for the emergency department? Does the hospitalist respond to internal code functions within the institution? Does the hospitalist team offer any support for specialized inpatient units like obstetrics or mental health or the surgical area? Does the hospitalist group support any telephonic or telemedicine call function that is advisory, in addition to his or her in-house duties?
7. Define areas of nontraditional support. Does the hospitalist teach residents? Does the hospitalist cover the clinics or other ambulatory areas?
8. Define any unique accreditation or quality support or credentialing functions. Does the hospitalist team have a specific function or status within the medical staff structure? Is the hospitalist team represented on any credentialing committee or any quality assurance function? How are hospitalists credentialed?
9. Define the compensation structure. Does the hospitalist unit bill for, and keep, revenues from the patients the hospitalists see and treat? Is the hospitalist group supported by an exclusivity arrangement or other type of contractual provision that has a clear business value? How does the hospitalist group determine its charge to the hospital or the health system for coverage?

Measurement of Hospitalist Productivity and Quality and Value

There are several data points that can be applied to a hospitalist team. Chief among them is the basic coverage standards defined in the previous section. What is the coverage pattern? What is covered? What functions are performed? Who does the billing and who gets the revenue from patient encounters? Once these questions are asked, the standard parameters of performance can be applied.

- Are there any measures of patient satisfaction and referral satisfaction that can be used as a benchmark for performance?
- Are there any measures of patient effectiveness or quality of care that can be applied?
- Are there any productivity measures that need to be considered?

Patient and referral satisfaction are easily measured, and entire books can be written regarding what to measure and how to measure it. Generally, hospitals are already in the patient satisfaction measurement mode, and the incorporation of a hospitalist component is an easy adjustment to make to present surveys. Enlightened hospitals will employ the concept of a 360°-style evaluation tool* to encourage nursing staff and referring physicians and, possibly, other hospital departments to judge the effectiveness of the hospitalist service.

There are many benchmarks for productivity. Among them, the following are the most common:

- The general census as defined by the number of patients "carried" by the team or overseen by an individual within the team
- The number of RVUs† or work relative value units derived from the contact reports or billing reports or the medical management system employed by the health system
- Number of admissions (as counted by completed H&Ps—history and physical exams)
- Number of patient discharges
- Number and type of procedures performed
- Number of patients seen and discharged without admission (emergency department consults)
- Number of inpatient or departmental consults

If there are any other special features of the contract, they can be included in the process of measurement also. However, the main issue of contracting and deploying hospitalists may be the challenge of determining how well they perform. Are they adding any value to the process of patient care? Do the discharges enhance or improve length of stay? Does the discharge rate of the hospitalist team reflect a medical discharge process that is comparable to best practices when issues like readmission and post-hospital rehabilitation are taken into the equation?

As the traditional medical staff function continues to evolve, the contracting and management processes associated with hospitalists and the definition of how their coverage is defined will continue to emerge. Their involvement in health systems that are developing accountable care organizations (ACOs) and in the care of patients with chronic diseases will become more pronounced. The process of coverage of an inpatient event was once coordinated by a family physician and the

* This is a common human resources (HR) tool that employs feedback from customers, coworkers, supervisors, and subordinates to judge a person's performance. It is used in most large companies, and it has both proponents and detractors. The usage here is only to suggest that a hospitalist program has many sources of satisfaction that can be important beyond just the patient.

† The resource-based relative value scale (RBRVS) is a measure of physician productivity that has been adapted by most agencies that measure physician productivity. The best resource for beginning research on this topic is provided by the American Medical Society. http://www.ama-assn.org/ama/pub/physician-resources/solutions-managing-your-practice/coding-billing-insurance/the-resource-based-relative-value-scale.page?

transition was seamless from one phase of care to the next, in or out of the hospital. As the care became more complex and efficiency demanded that the hospital coordinate inpatient care, there became a challenge of managing the transition from one location of care to the next. This process is still being studied, and it is becoming obvious to some researchers that integration is suffering as the chasm between outpatient and inpatient care widens. This will mean that new quality measures will emerge and that the relationships will continue to be defined on a general basis, and that contracting, in specific environments, will have to be flexible and based within the planning context of the health care system and its other developmental initiatives.

Future metrics will most certainly include coordination functions within ambulatory care environments, articulation with post-discharge services, criteria for the certification of readmission rates, impact of patient cost per admission, and the oversight of a variety of cost containment functions. The hospitalist program is also a significant source of intelligence on any number of other departments and functions and on the efficiencies of various components of the medical staff. Any health care system that is not using its hospitalist team to gather market intelligence is truly wasting a valuable resource.

Job Description—Hospitalist (Internal Medicine)*

Qualifications

- Board certified in internal medicine
- Minimum 3 years practice experience in the Borough of Queens
- Member of New York Physicians' Network
- Excellent medical records documentation skills
- Excellent communication skills and rapport with Queens colleague physicians

Relationships

Reports to the medical director, physician-hospital organization as part of the internal medicine service.

Description of Hospitalist/Internal Medicine Service Objectives

- To employ only highly skilled and qualified internal medicine physicians who have established private offices in the borough for which they provide medical inpatient coverage

* A variety of job descriptions are available for use by readers of this book at www.medicalstaffintegration.org.

- To cost-effectively provide inpatient medical coverage for patients
- To standardize, in any appropriate manner, the care to be provided to inpatients without compromising the ability of the internal medicine service (IMS) physicians and the referring physicians to make independent patient care decisions as necessary
- To improve the quality of inpatient care
- To promote continuity of care from the outpatient to the inpatient and back to the outpatient setting by enhancing and improving communication between the IMS and the referring physicians
- To gain the confidence and support of the referring physician community for the IMS
- To offer referring physicians a highly qualified alternative to inpatient rounding that meets the medical standards of the community

Responsibilities of Hospitalist/Internal Medicine Physicians

- To work closely with the emergency department staff physicians to take over the care of patients who must be admitted on behalf of the referring physicians who are participating in the IMS.
- To provide, at a minimum, daily rounding on IMS patients throughout the admission.
- To provide detailed history and physical examinations proximal to the time of admission, discharge assessments, daily hospital assessments, and consultations for all IMS patients. Must meet current Medicare and other third-party payer documentation guidelines in charting all medical care provided.
- To communicate regularly with the patient's physician, either by telephone, in person, or in writing (facsimile, letter, chart note, etc.), to provide him or her with current medical information and an opportunity to exchange pertinent history and findings.
- To coordinate the flow of paperwork with staff regarding all of the following matters:
  - Admission notification to the referring physician
  - Status report on patient, at a minimum of every 3 days, to the referring physician
  - Notification of discharge plan, including coordination of the discharge follow-up required
  - Preparation and submission of all necessary billing documentation and records
- During the hours of 9:00 a.m. to 5:00 p.m., Monday through Friday, the IMS physician on call will respond to the hospital (floor or emergency room) to provide admission services for patients referred either through the emergency room or directly by the referring physician's

office. Response time to the hospital for admission during these hours will be 2 hours.

- At all other times, the IMS physician on call will be paged by hospital staff. The ER physician will review the case with the on-call physician, who will determine disposition and evaluate the patient personally within 8 hours of admission to the floor.
- Will participate in continuing education as required for his or her specialty and board status.

Example: RFI/RFP Scope of Work for a Hospital-Based Group (ED)*

This request for proposal (RFP) is not complete without the standard background statement, rules of submission, dates for responses, etc. However, the reason to include the scope of work here is to demonstrate that there is a set of standards that can be defined for an emergency department group beyond just "covering the department."

Emergency Department Provider Items/General Services

The provider group will be responsible for obtaining any permits, licenses, or credentialing approvals necessary for it (and its individual providers) to assure contract performance. This shall be done at its own expense. This includes the responsibility to have each medical staff person credentialed appropriately at the hospital and to assure that they understand that their privileges and credentialing process are coterminus with the emergency department contract.

All employees and personnel subcontracted at the hospital site will be hired by the provider group and will be independent from the hospital except as the resulting contract defines the relationship. No employee or subcontractor will have any restriction in his or her hire agreement or contract that prevents him or her from continuing to provide service at the hospital site following the termination of any contract with the provider group.

The provider group will be exclusive to the hospital in all matters related to emergency department services, and it will execute, and cause its hired and contracted providers to execute, a restrictive covenant and noncompetition agreement to that effect. The agreement will have the hospital as the beneficiary of the noncompetition and restrictive covenant arrangement, and nothing in the corporate structure of the provider group or in the contracts that it executes with its partners

---

* This RFP and others can be downloaded in document-ready format from www.medicalstaff-integration.org.

or hirelings or subcontractors will further restrict their contracting rights beyond the restrictions directly defined with the hospital.

The provider group will be responsible for obtaining, and maintaining, any insurance coverage necessary for the fulfillment of contract terms. This shall be done at its own expense, and it shall be inclusive of malpractice coverage (to the maximum obtainable in ______ [State] for emergency department services), general liability insurance, property and casualty insurance (to the limits suggested by the hospital under the contract terms), and workers' compensation. The provider group will also address the issue of "tail coverage" to the satisfaction of the hospital under this agreement and provide for this coverage, if necessary and at its own expense, for any physician hired or contracted to provide services under this agreement.

The provider group is responsible for providing its own benefits program and retirement program. The hospital will be informed of the programs that are in place for the contracted and hired providers supplied under this arrangement.

The provider group will suggest a doctor (or doctors) to act as the chief of emergency department services at the hospital and identify other physicians who can provide committee support as requested by the CMO. Once the CMO confirms his or her choice of the doctor to be appointed as the chief of the emergency department, the provider group will assign operational authority to that individual to act on behalf of the provider group to effect contract performance.

The provider group will maintain equipment and monitor its compliance with standards appropriate for each class or category of equipment and in compliance with the instructions from the original supplier. There will be an equipment inventory system and a process to assure that the equipment is safe for the use intended. The provider group will work with the hospital biomedical maintenance and certification processes to assure that equipment and maintenance meet/exceed all published applicable biomedical engineering and accreditation standards.

A licensed and qualified physician will be on the premises of the hospital within the emergency department 24 hours per day, 7 days per week to provide emergency services to the patients and clients of the emergency department services at the hospital.

The provider group will establish coverage for the physical environs of the emergency department and will staff the process of patient care from the point of initial contact to discharge from the department.

A schedule will be published that is doctor specific, and it will address not only the primary coverage arrangements, but also a physician-specific plan for peak loading in the department, with the primary goal of assuring optimization of patient access, safety, and satisfaction.

A charge physician will be identified for the ED management team, and that physician will be the party directly responsible for the direct management of the emergency medicine services component, including all staging areas that relate to the ED patient flow.

The provider group will ensure that there is a standard established for automatic triggering of additional physician support. A tracking process will be designed and implemented that incorporates continuous quality improvement processes to measure and assure the rate of patient flow and service response to a standard that assures that 90% of all patients presented in the department are seen by a physician within a 15-minute time period of their registration being completed. However, in no case will the queuing rate standard compromise the highest order of patient care and safety.

Providers will take an active role in assisting hospital staff in transitioning patients from one staging area of the care cycle to the appropriate area of care. However, in the case of patients who cannot be transferred, the provider group will assure that the patients are cared for in their transitional status by providing oversight for their care while still in the department, even though they may be post-discharge.

The provider group will develop a process to identify and track ED referrals, their source and disposition, to assure that the patients receive access to the best qualified specialty care associated with the hospital. This process will be handled in conjunction with the CMO or hospital.

The provider group will support the hospital in the management of patient access to other areas where diagnostic and treatment services can be rendered. This may involve providing professional oversight, reporting on deviations from standard practices, taking responsibility to notify administration concerning delays and access problems, etc.

The provider group will participate in the shift transition and in staff informational meetings between care teams in a fashion that is supportive of the ED staff and administration.

The provider group will provide a dedicated physician liaison to the preadmission testing (PAT) area to assist with the collection and completion of precase testing. This physician will assist PAT staff in providing requested information and resources to patients scheduled for procedures or cases at the hospital and to their physicians.

The provider group will maintain and monitor a call system for private attending staff members that is consistent with hospital policies. Reporting on staff and attending response to ED physician requests and the timing of the responses will be required information in any monthly summary of ED statistics.

The provider group will develop a set of key performance indicators (KPIs) that will allow collaboration between the hospital and the group to continue the improvement of the department and its service structure.

The provider group will regularly review the quality and efficiency of related support services (transport, radiology, laboratory, etc.) and work with the CMO and with the hospital leadership to assess the need for improvement.

The provider group will publish a practice policy, protocol, and procedure manual approved by the CMO.

The provider group will source and establish a program that assures that the care and the processes at the hospital are in keeping with the best practices referenced in available and pertinent research as it applies to the discipline of emergency department and all categories of care provided at the hospital through this contract.

The provider group will coordinate all call schedules and call protocols with the hospital administration to the satisfaction of the CMO. This includes detailing the status of the providers on call and maintaining a backup plan for coverage should initial levels of coverage become inadequate due to peak loading, disaster, or other unplanned events.

Emergency Department Provider Items/ Recruitment and Orientation

The provider group will keep comprehensive background records and employment records on each employee, and it will warrant to the hospital that each employee has been the subject of a criminal background check and meets acceptable risk standards relative to the provision of medical care. These records will be available for hospital review.

The provider group will assure that the emergency department team is consistent to the hospital (primarily assigned to the hospital and its service units) and that there is an in-place, in-use physician orientation plan approved by the hospital.

The provider group will demonstrate in-place, in-use processes for the development of a manpower planning and succession process that details the selection and replacement schedule for new physicians who will be assigned to staff areas defined in this agreement. The plan will be submitted to the CMO for review and approval.

The provider group will demonstrate a process for the evaluation of physicians and providers that is acceptable to the CMO. As part of this process, there will be a provision for the removal of a provider or a physician from the service roster at the hospital when that provider or physician is identified by the CMO as a provider who is noncompliant with the standards of care and service at the hospital.

The provider group will be incorporated or structured in a fashion that allows professional development through the advancement of hired physicians to partnership status within the provider group. This will be demonstrated by the incorporation of criteria for partner development and equity involvement within the corporate structure of the provider group in a fashion that is open to review by the hospital and is within standard norms for emergency department groups.

The provider group will develop, or provide for review, corporate documents that adequately address decision-making authority, corporate officers (including terms of services), physician disability, shareholder terminations, and practice limitations that complement the terms of service to the hospital. The provider group will coordinate its governance process with that of the hospital contract and will assure that this process is consistent with stipulations and assignments within this agreement.

The provider group will publish written job descriptions for all hired or contracted providers assigned to the hospital.

The provider group will enforce the terms of the agreement between the hospital and the provider group in all subcontracts with its vendors, suppliers, support personnel, employees, and physician staff (partnership status included).

The provider group will work with the CMO to develop a leadership development program for physicians who are placed in supervisory or leadership positions under this agreement.

Emergency Department Provider Items/Financial Services

The provider group will comply with all aspects of the criteria for managed care contracting for the plans and programs that are selected by the hospital for institutional participation.

The provider group will coordinate registration and billing efforts with the hospital and with any contractor chosen by the hospital to assure that timely and accurate billing and registration is accomplished.

The provider group will develop, in conjunction with the hospital, appropriate financial and cash handling functions related to the processing of billing and collection functions to hospital patients. This will include coordinated organization of bookkeeping standards, the reconciliation of explanation of benefit (EOB) reports, billing and collection reports, patient account write-offs, the development of financial benchmarking reports, and the reporting of charity care.

The provider group will demonstrate in-place, in-use patient accounts' dispute resolution processes approved by the hospital.

The provider group will maintain a lockbox relationship with a local bank acceptable to the hospital for the deposit of any funds collected on behalf of the provider group, and the provider group will participate actively in a timely reconciliation of billing reports and deposits that can be used to assure that posted accounts are accurate.

The provider group will maintain a certain level of charity services consistent with those provided by other members of the medical staff at the hospital in order to assure that cases that do not qualify for direct billing can be served at the hospital.

Emergency Department Provider Items/Compliance

The provider group will have a written quality assurance program with established monitoring, peer review, and corrective action plans that articulate with those of the hospital. One physician, satisfactory to the CMO, must be named as the QA officer and attend all meetings related to the QA and continuous quality improvement process.

The provider group will have an in-place, in-use compliance plan approved by the hospital and will name a compliance officer acceptable to the CMO. This compliance plan will address Health Insurance Portability and Accountability Act (HIPAA) and Emergency Medical Treatment and Active Labor Act (EMTALA) requirements.

The provider group will maintain responsibility for any accreditation or licensing function associated with, or complemented by, emergency department services. An accreditation officer will be named by the provider group who is acceptable to the CMO.

The provider group will maintain confidentiality in all aspects of this agreement and will establish a standard within its membership to maintain discretion, privacy, confidentiality, and professionalism with regard to internal group matters.

The provider group will demonstrate financial solvency through the provision of periodic opinions from relevant business advisors as may be requested from time to time by the hospital.

The provider group will develop and maintain a formal process for complaint investigation, communication, and resolution. This will be a process that articulates with the office of the CMO. The provider group will also coordinate its incident reporting processes with those of the hospital.

Example: Evaluation of a Contracted Group's Performance

See Table 9.1.

How often do you utilize the services of this division? Often? Occasionally? Seldom?

If you have received a complaint from your staff or a patient concerning the services of this division, could you generally describe the issue and its impact and implications?

Summary Issues

- Contracting for services is a process that is well done in the field of manufacturing but generally not very well done in the nonprofit hospital environment. Just engaging in this process can cause both parties to address quality and service issues and establish metrics that need to be defined when faced with a contractor that wants an integrated response to its contracting opportunity.
- Hospitals who ignore this important component of the medical staff may find that their own doctors are internally competitive with them when it comes time to contract externally. The inability to predict where a hospital-based group might stand in a contracting situation may mean that they command

Table 9.1 Evaluating the Contracted Provider Group

Criteria	*Strongly Disagree*	*Disagree*	*Agree*	*Strongly Agree*	*No Opinion*
The care provided meets or exceeds the community norm.					
The division is responsive to the needs of the medical staff.					
The physicians are courteous to my patients.					
The physicians adequately explain procedures before they commence.					
There are sufficient numbers of physicians to adequately and appropriately staff the division.					
The physicians are readily available for my patients.					
The hours of operation/ coverage are sufficient.					
The level of expertise or specialty mix among members of the division is appropriate.					
Procedures are scheduled and done without unreasonable delay.					
Interpretations are rendered in a timely manner, and they are easily incorporated within my electronic medical record (EMR) system.					

(Continued)

Table 9.1 Evaluating the Contracted Provider Group (Continued)

Criteria	*Strongly Disagree*	*Disagree*	*Agree*	*Strongly Agree*	*No Opinion*
The physicians are responsive to my suggestions.					
The department equipment is state of the art.					
The members of the group provide charity care when requested.					
The medical director is a team player. He or she seeks to cooperate with the chief medical officer, CEO, and other medical staff members and administrative staff.					
The medical director actively participates in meetings of the medical executive committee.					
The medical director actively participates in continuous quality improvement.					
The medical director supports and encourages cost-effective measures and procedures.					

a separate place at the negotiation table when population management and bundled pricing contracts are sought by managed care organizations.

- Hospitals generally believe that they have little or no leverage. This is not the case. There are any number of avenues for fulfilling contract service roles, and in some cases, the specialists themselves are fragmented. An exclusive contract for the coverage of a hospital department or service line has great value, and it should be something that is managed like any other resource.

- The integration of fee schedules for contracting is challenging. The hired doctor on a contract is immune from contract terms that are generated by external negotiation, while the independent group that contracts with a hospital may be fully exposed. The goal of a common contracting platform has to be constantly kept in the forefront of any contract discussion.

Chapter 10

Sponsored Practices and Hired Practitioners (Employment)

Employment seems to be the model of choice right now. That is probably because it has none of the issues that are present with the other models. The practice is purchased, and the doctors go to work for the health system. There is money up front for the physicians, and they sidestep future risk except for the risk of working for a hospital, which is certainly not risk-free, but it is at least a risk that is defined in a contract. The hospital gains an integral part of its medical staff complement in a form that is pretty dependable, and it is a form that has fewer compliance issues and lower overall maintenance (at least as far as governance is concerned). The doctor is often able to free capital from the practice that can be put to use now and be released from long-term debt in an uncertain business environment. Generally, both parties can complete the transactions involved without the tedious negotiations and external considerations that group formation (independent provider associations (IPAs), physician-hospital organizations (PHOs), management services organizations (MSOs)) would demand.

Simple, But Many Moving Parts

The principles of practice acquisition are simple, but there are a number of components, and any hospital may manage all of these across a broad bureaucratic spectrum every day. However, the practice purchase must bring all of the hospital resources into focus on a single transaction or group of transactions, and this may take a different approach or a reorganized structure. The following people, or their departments, have to be working as one in order to bring the transaction to a place where it can be negotiated and more importantly, once negotiated, managed.

- Finance
- Reimbursement and billing
- IT
- Human resources
- Compliance (coding)
- Property management
- Ancillary services support
- Medical staff office
- Legal affairs

All of these people interrelate daily, but the effective team needs to be structured more like something designed by a general in the field than by a politician. This is the type of project activity that would be best handled if it were under the direction of a single person, or an office that is dedicated to the one function of practice acquisition and reengineering. Some hospitals are starting to call this function onboarding, which is a term that a cruise ship might use to describe bringing excited and willing passengers onboard in an orderly fashion. Bringing a physician practice into a health care bureaucracy is something entirely different.

One might argue that the many outpatient units that a hospital sponsors operate like a physician practice. However, the clinics, emergency department, urgent care centers, etc., are not a perfect fit model on which to base the incorporation of a private practice run by independent physicians to one that is going to be transformed to a hospital-based practice. This is a good place to look for similar functions and support mechanisms, but the cultures are very different. It is a mistake to assume that outpatient service units that have been crafted to fit within the hospital administrative structure can provide a model that can be overlaid effectively to manage a group of sites that were once managed by autocratic physicians in private practices.

To Every Project, a Process

In order to be successful, one must first define success. It is not evident to all of the parties in a practice sale how the features of the sale and the resulting transaction might be perceived by the other party. One should carefully define or develop a rationale that supports the overall idea of this transaction and which describes the advantages generally to each entity. This part of the process is more for the parties to gain an understanding of the position of each and the needs and philosophical base on which the transaction is based. Essentially, why are we doing this? More important, why are *they* doing this?

From the hospital perspective, this cannot be for referrals or for the development of additional volume. This is not a book about compliance issues, but the facts of a transaction cannot be based upon a shift of patients from one institution to another. This behavior can be quickly defined under regulatory sanctions, and all of the parties will be subject to sanction, and worse. However, a hospital has any number of reasons to purchase physician practices, and many of them are defensible and easily defended from a business case perspective. Some are listed below:

Continued development of economics of scale
Development to serve an underserved patient base
Improved coordination of patient care
Enhanced ability to recruit physicians of a needed discipline
Coordination of assets and capital
Improved information linkages
Improved ability to serve a specific geographic region
Reduction of risk in contracting under managed care
Improvement of integrated health system development

One assumes that the physician is doing the deal to achieve some better place than what a private practice can provide—from an economic and a lifestyle perspective. This includes reduction of risk and access to embedded capital within the practice and a reasonable employment contract. Lifestyle matters may address call responsibilities, changes in governance, release from operational issues, etc. Many doctors state simply that they just want to practice medicine and not be exposed to the everyday hassles of managing an office. Most cite new regulations and the need for additional capital and overhead associated with electronic medical records. Certainly, there is a factor that relates to the fear of the unknown future that health care payment reform will bring as contracting forms change.

If either party is convinced that this new structure will be the same as everything has been in the past, only better, then there is a disconnect that should be corrected. Unrealistic expectations will produce disappointment and will result in continued negotiation after the transaction is complete. The fact is that everything is changing, and this is a new relationship that might assist each party in undergoing these changes in a more calm and programmed fashion. This is about reducing risk for the physician and removing the doctors from a market for which they are unprepared, and it is a mechanism for the hospital to gain stability in market share and to be able to command a unit of production that can contract under a new set of rules.

Structure—Pick One

What will be the *structure* of the resulting entity? Will the doctors be hired directly into the hospital system or will it be a sponsored professional corporation (PC) with some independence? Will there be a related management services organization or clinic responsibilities? What characteristics of each will support the goals that have been agreed upon? If an MSO is determined, the structure of services and the relative costs must be defined since they will have some kind of impact on the practices that are being reorganized. If there is to be a purchase of assets and employment of physicians, relative price and employment issues must be addressed. Most important, under any formal model, there must be some element of physician involvement in governance.

Form follows function with respect to finances. On each side of the transaction, some kind of financial feasibility must be performed to assure that the arrangement meets standards of fiscal prudence for everyone involved. All parties must be confident that appropriate due diligence has been conducted to allow full disclosure of any pending liabilities and potential risk. In each case, these issues are more straightforward from the physician perspective. Most deals will be reduced to a price for assets and an employment arrangement. The only risk question may be how long the contract might be and what stipulations there are for separation. Other chapters in this book will deal with the many issues that can arise with physician contract form and income distribution.

Governance deserves special mention. Some kind of process must be determined that will allow the doctors to retain control over medical matters while allowing principals of the health system to maintain jurisdiction and stewardship over financial issues. This process should somehow mirror the traditional culture of the practice being acquired. Discussions should be very precise over operational issues vs. governance issues, and the most important aspect of any decision process should be the clear definition of who has the final say in any category. Of course, the doctor has purview over medical issues, but there can be a wide-ranging discussion about what is medical when it comes to staffing and equipment and supplies. These are areas where the private practitioner is giving up some power to a process, and that process has to incorporate some reasonable level of input from the physicians if it is to have any credibility and support.

The decision-making prerogatives of an individual physician must be preserved and balanced with the long-term planning needs of the overall organization. Decisions that might be collaborative must be discussed to assure that they are made at the appropriate management level and with the proper amount of communication and consensus.

The role of the management staff at the group level and its relationship to the main organization must also be explored. This is where an organization chart should be introduced to define relationships and, most important for the development team, the areas of potential overlap with other departments within the organization. If possible, job descriptions (even in abbreviated formats) should be developed for any position on the organizational chart, especially if they are to be held by a physician. If committees are determined to be necessary, their role should be carefully defined by outlining their scope and purpose. People have a job description, and committees should have their own defined role that is delineated beyond just the name of the committee.

Transactions and Transaction Elements

Without restating the process that goes into the decision to sell a practice, the components of the sale have been outlined below to serve as a checklist against which the reader can develop his or her own listing and assign each area to someone on the deal team that can address it.

1. Assuming a sale of assets is to occur, they need to be valued and a determination made about how that value is going to be defined for tax purposes.
2. There have to be physician employment agreements that define the term of employment and the compensation methodology.
3. If productivity is a part of the methodology, there has to be a baseline data for physician production.
4. A component of any agreement is the restrictive covenants or noncompete. These can range from simple to complex, narrow or broad, but they are always present in some form.
5. If a physician is to be allowed activity at other hospitals, this should be outlined.
6. Insurance "tail" or "prior acts" coverage for physicians must be clarified as a transaction unfolds.
7. The physicians' office space and support requirements must be reviewed, especially if they are to be related to contractual items.
8. If there are issues related to the physicians holding medical staff credentials or gaining department-level privileges, these have to be defined.
9. If there are "unwind" provisions in the existing physician corporation or organization, these may need to be addressed.
10. Changing Medicare and other third-party payer contracts may require a lead time for notification. This issue will also have some impact on cash flow since the lag in transition from one plan to another may mean that some claims cannot be immediately processed. This is one area that will have a major impact on the financial projections and *pro forma* of any medical practice division.
11. If there are other state and federal requirements and procedures, they must be identified and addressed. One that comes to mind that might have an impact is the issue of certificate of need (CON). In some states, there is an approval

process that must be addressed in order to complete any major financial transaction. This will include many physician practice purchases.
12. Any closure of the former practice has to address existing physician employment agreements as well as pension plans and benefits. Most of the issues can be addressed very easily, but someone has to be assigned to make sure that everything is coordinated to make sure that there is no lack of coverage.
13. If a transfer of medical records is appropriate, this may need to be coordinated to assure that all Health Insurance Portability and Accountability Act (HIPAA) regulations are accommodated. It seems unlikely that any problems might occur with a physician that is transferring from one entity to another, but if other doctors remain in the former practice, there could be some question over the ability to transfer records, and this must be defined prior to any action that would be seen as alienating the patients or compromising medical privacy.
14. Not only do patients need to be transitioned, but there also has to be some attention paid to the existing accounts receivable (AR) of the practice. If they are to remain in the ownership of the doctors, then the billing and collection will have to be organized in some fashion that minimizes patient confusion. This is a process that is often mismanaged by hospitals that want to ignore the past AR and simply let the physicians collect them on their own. This will be in the best interests of the hospital billing staff, but it will not serve the patients well as they begin to get billings for service from their doctor from two different sources and, when they attempt to resolve issues at the physician's office (the new office), are faced with staff who have only one part of the record or who only care about collecting for the hospital.
15. If an MSO arrangement or a sale of assets is to occur, that will have implications for structural reorganization that involves leases, employees, and capital equipment. Most vendor arrangements will also have to be redone. If there is a conversion of employees from one organization to another, they have to be notified and the conversion managed to minimize any unintended consequences.
16. Whatever the form that results, there has to be an overall salary reclassification and the placement of employees within some level of classification that matches other practices and, hopefully, has some parity with the health care system.

Whatever the end result, the process associated with the valuation and the transaction must be handled by counsel who are familiar with this type of a deal and who are involved in compliance matters on a routine basis. The greatest challenge is not striking a deal. Uninformed parties get together on a regular basis and discuss "what if" scenarios all the time. Getting from that initial discussion to a final document execution is the part that takes some experience and guidance. Some health systems have a team approach and a standard set of policies that can be applied when a doctor becomes interested in selling a practice. This is the most defensible and businesslike approach to the process. There is a policy statement in the appendix that can be used as a reference point, but the following process is generally followed.

- Initial meeting and broad agreements are reached between the hospital and the doctors.
- A letter of intent (LOI) is crafted and executed along standard health system guidelines. An NDA is also executed. The LOI contains a specific timeline for document development and execution.
- Information is received from the practice that contains financial and operational statistics. This includes material regarding employees, capital equipment, vendor relationships, etc.
- If real estate, benefits programs, and insurance matters (including malpractice) are going to be reorganized, there is a separate process for determining how they will be transitioned.
- An internal (health system) *pro forma* is developed that makes the business case internally for the proposed transaction. A statement of value proposition is also crafted for the doctors that explains the way the deal will impact each of them on a personal level.
- The parties meet again to endorse the initial planning and progress related to the transaction. At this stage, the health system and the doctors have completed their individual due diligence on the proposed arrangement. And at this stage, before contracts are developed, a determination is made whether there is any appetite to move forward. The timeline is adjusted to reflect a closing date that can be used for transition, assuming the parties move forward.
- Contracts are developed. Fair market value assessments are commissioned from outside consultants, if necessary. External vendors and internal hospital support departments (HR, compliance, coding, medical records, etc.) are engaged and advised to prepare for the transactional elements that will be specific to their interests.
- If necessary and indicated, appropriate health care committees are advised and approvals are confirmed.
- Contract review results, hopefully, in closure around the original LOI—and the arrangement is scheduled for execution.

Only when this process is fully in place and moving toward a final date should the employees be engaged and the process become more public. If there are any prior discussions among support staff, there could be some level of erosion among key employee groups that are necessary for project success.

No one contract among the many that are necessary is more complex, from a business perspective. The challenge is often to make sure that a key agreement is not forgotten or left as an "orphan" part of the arrangement. Some of the areas that are often forgotten include key employee contracts, software licenses, service agreements, intellectual property assignments (especially those that relate to the

Internet), license agreements for billing and collections, etc. The best way to collect any and all agreements that a practice has in place is to look at a chart of accounts and the backup material in the trial balance that comprises it. This material should be reviewed along with credit card statements and contract files to assure that everything that has a subscription fee of some sort is tracked.

Special Circumstances—Normalizing Practice Numbers

Most practices report on an annual basis (calendar year), and they do their bookkeeping to optimize tax treatment. Sometimes, bookkeeping is based on a ledger and account system that is not really traditional for medical practices. In studying these practices, the financial material first needs to be normalized. That means it must be put in a form that is consistent with national benchmarks and with other practices that are sponsored by the health care organization. Sometimes it means "teasing out" some of the costs that are actually of direct benefit to the physician-owners who characterize them differently than a health care system might.

The challenges increase if the physician has any number of contracts or cash flow arrangements that are derived from outside the practice that might be impacted by the proposed arrangement. This could mean anything from taking cash in the practice from co-pays and deductibles as unreported income to having book royalties or expert witness pay. Most health care systems and group practices and organized groups described in this book will require, at the least, that clinical revenues be channeled through the arrangement that is being negotiated.

The terminology is "all time and all effort," and the concept is that if the malpractice arrangement is supposed to cover the activity of the doctors, then the doctors have to be doing all of that activity for the party that provides the main contractual coverage. However, this is really an oversimplification since there are other factors that come into the issue when a doctor is in the community representing some position or treatment that might be controversial; this might be restricted. A physician that has been recruited by a parochial institution may not be free to work in a setting that provides services that are against the principles of that organization, for example (think of all of the issues that surround freedom of choice and right to life). There is also the example of the practice that is involved in a product endorsement arrangement or a research situation that is outside any arena that the sponsoring institution might tolerate (image enhancement services, alternative medicine).

Special Circumstances—Asset vs. Stock Purchase

The simple answer is that the hospital wants to purchase assets only and the doctor wants to sell the entire business. That is, unless the doctor wants to do something like leasing the business or venturing in some other unique way. These more exotic options are explored elsewhere in this book. In this section, we recognize two primary options: a transaction involving stock (the business enterprise) and a transaction that is defined by the practice assets.

Why does the hospital want to purchase assets? The reasons relate to the dependability of the fair market value assessment and the limitation of risk. Any organization that has been in business for any length of time has some sort of undiscovered liability lurking within the fabric of its past. The following listing suggests the ones that come immediately to mind:

- Unquantified risk relating to employment matters like Equal Employment Opportunity Commission (EEOC) claims or wage and hour claims
- Unquantified risk relating to employee perception of harassment or mistreatment
- Unpaid vendor claims and liabilities
- Partnership and shareholder claims
- Undiscovered malpractice liability
- Billing/coding and claims processing matters
- Coding audits—specific to providers
- Unmet or undiscovered maintenance issues
- Pending or unfiled civil infractions, tax penalties, etc.

These liabilities can be avoided altogether with a pure asset purchase. However, the physician may have compelling tax reasons to sell the stock of the practice, and he or she will also want to avoid undiscovered liabilities. There may be a transaction that fits within a nonprofit organization if there can be some definition of risk and some way to prevent that risk from being transferred in a fashion that is open-ended to the hospital. Counsel can assist with the development of withhold accounts that can be held in escrow until such time as the health system can be reasonably assured that there is no further risk. There can also be an audit prior to execution that could assist the parties with understanding risk, although this approach is less desirable.*

Special Circumstances—Leasing Practices

So, maybe the hospital should just lease the practice? This is a simple structure with complex and far-reaching implications. The concept is that the doctors would receive salaries, or salaries and an opportunity for a bonus, and the practice would not be purchased but would be leased for a period of time. This means that

* One way to audit EEOC liability is to ask employees if they think that they have a claim. This has some risk because it encourages them to focus on EEOC standards, and the action of the survey may be to actually surface a claim that would have otherwise gone undiscovered. A coding and billing audit that discovers past errors or mistakes in coding also requires self-reporting in many cases. While it is not necessarily best not to know, it is sometimes best to do prospective review rather than to try to find errors in the existing billing files.

everything stays in place and under the same structure (except for the doctors). One might think of the leasing company (the doctors who own the practice and its components) as an independent build-to-suit contractor that simply owns a site and all of the material and employees that go with it. One monthly fee covers the access to the site and the hospital simply provides the doctors.

However, leasing must be constructed on a basis of a fair market value determination. Simply having one of the parties come up with a price for a practice lease is not going to give the development team a standard for a transaction. The price must be determined independently and from an objective perspective. The problem is that the doctors who own the components of production of the practice (employees, real estate, equipment, etc.) often have a vaulted price in mind for these, and they may have been working with schedules for salaries and leases that do not meet the test of fair market review.

Another reason that the parties choose a practice lease situation might be to allow the doctors to return to private practice if things do not work out. This also seems like a simple and straightforward concept. Keep the components of the practice together and lease them to the hospital with the idea that the lease can be canceled at some future point in time, and the practice will be intact and the doctors can return to their traditional practice environment. This is somewhat impractical since things in a practice change and employees turn over. Changes that have been capitalized by the hospital will have to be recovered when, and if, the practice is returned to the doctors following the lease. If the lease is converted to a sale at some future point, the capitalization of things like an electronic medical record (EMR) or new furnishings will have to be taken into account.

Special Circumstances—Fractional Purchase

A fractional purchase is the purchase of a share of the stock or a portion of a partnership in a limited liability professional corporation. Buying part of a practice is more complex than buying the practice since there are implications for governance and decision making that the hospital may have to have coordinated with the transaction. In other words, certain aspects of the purchase may be unconventional because the hospital, especially if it is a nonprofit entity or a sponsored institution, will have to have some precise guarantees that extend beyond the nature of the portion of stock or partnership that it has purchased. Examples might be related to participation in managed care plans, coverage for indigent populations, participation in Medicaid, etc. The guarantees will also state how new partners might be added (especially institutional partners), and in the case of organizations that have sponsorship from a religious institution, there may be issues related to what types of services might be offered.*

Another type of fractional purchase may be the idea of the hospital purchasing only a defined component of the practice—say, the diagnostic services component or the rehab services. In this case, there can be more distinct separation of governance, and the whole transaction can be based on standard business processes. There are, of course, regulatory and compliance constraints that will impact the business decision. The practice may own a rehabilitation unit that can be segmented out and sold to a hospital, but counsel associated with hospitals will advise their clients that they cannot buy the unit and guarantee continued referrals. One solution to this might be to also purchase a noncompete commitment from the practice and the doctors. This would, at the very least, assure that the doctors will not be developing another unit that will attract their referrals. Again, counsel may need to weigh in on this type of a transaction along with valuation consultants to assure that the hospital is not duplicating a payment for the business along with a payment for a noncompete.

Special Circumstances—Related Parties

Related parties come in all shapes and sizes. They have to be identified and their impact insulated from any potential arrangement. Among the most common is the practice that has employees that are formally or informally or formerly related to one of the physicians. Any good operational manager who honestly reflects upon his or her experience and whatever common sense he or she has developed in managing people will point out that nepotism never works out. From the perspective of normalizing costs, the related employee is generally paid off-scale and may have some advantageous benefits or scheduling privileges that other employees do not enjoy. The best manager for a physician in a practice that he or she owns may be the spouse, but the transition from private practice to integrated practice will require that the manager be relocated to another management opportunity, if qualified.

Related party issues also arise when there is an ownership interest in a building, consulting firm, or an MSO that provides space, equipment, or services to the practice. There are many reasons that a physician might rent from a family-owned corporation or form an MSO to provide services. These types of structures are used in tax and estate planning to move money that might otherwise be taxed as income

* The most obvious are the hospitals related to the Catholic faith in some way. These institutions would have to have some acknowledgment to the *Ethical and Religious Directives for Catholic Health Care Services* published by the U.S. Conference of Catholic Bishops. These will define end-of-life care and women's care issues, and the most recent edition also addresses how Catholic-sponsored organizations can enter into partnerships with lay organizations and physicians. http://www.usccb.org/about/doctrine/ethical-and-religious-directives/.

to an arena where it will receive more favorable treatment. It also allows a physician to title some assets in a corporation that benefits family members who might be taxed at a lower rate. A building or real estate or equipment can also be owned by nonphysicians like a practice manager or physician family members. All of these relationships have purpose in an estate planning function or in personal tax strategy, but they are an impediment in a sale.

Special Circumstances—Underwater Practice

Borrowing a term from real estate, some practices are just plain "underwater," and the transaction that is necessary to achieve some kind of integration with a hospital might be bankruptcy. However, this is generally not thought of as practical or political to suggest. The practice that is saddled with debt or which has tax obligations or which is structured with retiring partners can often simply not make it from one year to the next while retaining its hold on newly recruited physicians and meeting the needs of the principals for some kind of competitive salary.

The warning signs of a practice in trouble, besides the obvious ones that are present when there is a simple cash flow crunch, are many. Look for retired partners and an obligation on the books to fund buy-outs. Check the income and expense statements for trends in income that are negative or for large year-end loans to pay bonuses. Look for staff and physician turnover or for any cash or collection process that would not be considered mainstream.

The challenge with this type of a practice is that the physicians have taken to this level one small step at a time. It is not their fault to have tried too hard to provide conventional services in a traditional structure using time-honored methods. The short-term goal is to educate them on the real options that they face and to assist them in moving through the steps to allow them to maintain services to their patients and to emerge in a better place.

The hospital cannot bail them out, loan them money, assume their debt, advance them bonus funds, factor their AR, or otherwise act to repair damages from years past. Clever consultants working with courageous lawyers may advance a number of alternative methods, but the fact remains that an integrated result has to be based upon present services and future earnings, not past expenses.

Some things that the hospital might do in an advisory capacity would be to offer suggestions on consulting assistance, assist with the capitalization (through an independent bank) of practice assets, work with counsel to define ways that might offset some expenses through the development of MSO contracts, etc.

Summary Issues

- Practice purchases take many forms, but the one central idea is that the doctor moves from a structure of total control and independence to one where governance is shared and structures are more bureaucratic. This is a major shift in a paradigm that is little understood by hospitals and hospital managers.
- There are many opportunities for physician equity reorganization (purchasing practices), but there are few good opportunities unless the process is planned and based on solid business principles. The hospital should be actively building a network from among a selected group or practitioners—not acquiring practices from doctors who simply want to sell them.
- Hospitals should contemplate the structure and choose the one form that works and qualify it internally before launching the process of acquisition. Impractical? Probably. If the process is already underway, then the hospital should put the process on hold while it considers the best or desired structure for acquired physicians.
- Specialty practices are different than primary care. There might be a case made that there could be a couple of different structures for acquired practice assets—one that complements a specialist and one that fosters the growth and nurturing of primary care.
- The more independent of hospital structure that the practice management staff and functions can be, the more successful they will be. This may seem like a "disintegrative"" statement, but solid experience as a hospital administrator does not assure good management of the physician practice enterprise. Processes and support functions that work for an institution often do not translate well to an office environment.

Chapter 11

Align the Correct Solution Supported by Effective Communications

If a hospital seeks a unified response with its medical staff to a health care payer system that is coalescing around many new forms of contracting,* more integration is better than less. The same goes for doctors, but they have a different perspective since they may have any number of choices based on their practice discipline and their time horizon left to practice. Why go through a transition that is costly and complex when one option may be to simply practice out to the end of a career and drop the keys on the carpet as you exit the building? Longevity and position in a market are different for a hospital than for a physician. Both need to operate from some kind of plan or vision of where they want to be in the near-term future.†

* These new forms are coming through structures like affordable care organizations (ACOs) and Centers for Medicare and Medicaid Services (CMS) and other groups that are rediscovering forms of capitation and population management and bundled pricing. Each market is moving at its own pace from traditional fee for service to something else. Generally, this "something else" will have a different contracting platform that transfers more risk to the providers and attempts to measure something that is not now measured—like quality or efficiencies or some other metric that cannot be done by any one set of providers.

† Long-term planning aside, health care delivery is a response to near-term needs. Capital that a hospital develops is certainly a longer-term decision, but many of the different aspects of this book surround short-term and near-term development. Planning horizons of 4 to 5 years are challenging for anyone in health care. Other authors, the futurists mentioned in the introduction, can look out 20 and 30 years to a different place, but without a near-term plan, the readers of this book will not be around that long.

Planning should address the overall position of the health care system in the marketplace and the mission of the health system. Does the health system actually respect and follow its mission? Does it have a shared vision with those that it serves? What does the system stand for that is in any way remarkable? Can any guiding principles be enshrined on the wall for all to see? If we put them up (probably on a website and not on the wall), would others understand them and endorse them to patients, families, and friends?

Planning is easy to talk about and hard to do. Consultants have a bag of tools that they use to elicit responses from clients so that they can order their own perspective and advice that they can hand back in a typed and bound document. Actually, in the best of cases, the consultant acts as a facilitator and a scribe and the client does all of the planning. If the overall plan is not available, and if there is not any consultant around to bark at the core group demanding that they list SWOTs* and key goals, that is okay. Some of the best plans are those that are homemade and hand crafted.

Here are some basics that can be addressed in order to structure some kind of framework in which the proposed physician transactions (and any resulting enterprises) can be judged. One starts with a basic assumption that the hospital, whatever its mission or vision, needs to stabilize the relationship with key physician practices and disciplines so that it can maintain some type of solid and risk-controlled financial performance.

That being said, the following areas must be understood:

- Review traditional area admission rates within the organization and compare them to those reported by competitors.
- Develop a model of "institutional loyalty" for the medical staff related to the organization. The goal is to begin to identify key medical staff based upon actual utilization of the resources.
- Using the referral and admission/discharge data, develop a crude ranking of growing, declining, and stable disciplines and the doctors connected to each.
- Define local demographic shift and proposed growth, and attempt to model population relative to the practice sites and the service area of the organization for the near term (5 years) and the long term (10 years).
- Apply some type of ranking to define present (stable) and growing medical franchises and to develop a listing of key stakeholders in the medical community that might have an impact upon the growth process in some functional fashion.
- Match specific practices to product lines and payer groups and patient groups that are of critical need for the institution.

---

* SWOTs refers to the development of a listing of an organization's strengths, weaknesses, opportunities, and threats. This is an exercise that many planning consultants go through to obtain background information and buy-in from a client when they are doing strategic planning.

- Where possible, sort the listing based upon traditional loyalty factors and likelihood of conversion of the practice to a more formal working relationship. This may involve segmenting by age, gender, ethnicity, etc.
- Determine, using realistic estimates, what level of capital and staff support is available to recruit the practices to some form of relationship with the organization. Set some kind of time and capital and physician limit.
- Rank the practices by their importance and strategic value.
- Develop standards and policies for the approach and overture to the target practices.* This is simply a script.

The "opportunities" will be coming at hospitals in a steady stream over the next few years, and the danger is that there will be no discerning process to sort what is an actual opportunity and what might be a potential waste of very limited resources. The questions must be framed with the answers already outlined. "We incorporate practices and physicians into the health system that complement our overall goal of serving the health care needs of patients and consumers in the greater Chickaming Township region when they are strong practices with physicians who command a solid position in the communities that we serve." Many hospitals behave as if their policy statement might be represented as: "We take on anything that comes through the door and we figure it all out later."

The last analogy in this section is that many hospitals sometimes take on practices like one would play gin rummy, which is a card game where there is a constant search for the right cards and cards are passed from player to player by discarding and hoping for a better match of some kind in the next round. However, physician-hospital integration is more like a game of bridge where you play the hand that you are dealt with a partner, and many times, the communication and collaboration of the partnership can allow a set of weaker cards to beat the opponent's stronger hand. With the right partner and the proper communications and by sharing a strategic vision, the hospital with bad luck and a weaker hand can win in health care development.

The Team Must Have a Shared Set of Principles and Core Values

No matter where the organization is based, no matter the market, there are some principles that always seem to surface. Planning by a consultant generally allows these to surface in some form of dialogue. Why waste the time? Just take a look at some of these and incorporate them within the core pieces of the plan where they

* A sample policy is included in the appendix that can be used as a start for developing some form of core ideas for practice acquisitions. There is also an administrative position description that may be helpful in outlining job responsibilities for a key staff member in the process.

fit. They are pretty standard for a health care organization, but they are worthy of discussion with physician business partners. It is imperative to get the basics out and on the table at the beginning of the development process.

1. The enterprise* will encompass all physicians' functions associated with the network.
2. The enterprise will assume medical control over all functions that are concerned with traditional medical staff duties related to the patients that are served. This includes any credentialing, accreditation, certification, or quality assurance functions.
3. Performance standards associated with the enterprise will be defined by national standards, and benchmarks will be established that are referenced against both internal and external measures.
4. All health care delivery functions—either hospital inpatient or outpatient—will be incorporated within the span of control of the enterprise. This includes patient experiences in the physician practice environments, the emergency department (ED), the inpatient units, the procedural units, and the recovery/rehab phases.
5. Integration standards for the patient cohort under the auspices of the enterprise will be coordinated throughout the patient experience through the use of a single registration function and a unified patient medical record.
6. The enterprise will be able to act on behalf of the provider's contract with managed care programs (including ACOs and insurance exchanges) as a single agent. This implies the capability to contract for capitated services, shared risk contracts, and bundled services.
7. Enterprise-related physicians will be fully engaged in all programming to assure that there is a seamless patient care experience related to any point at which the patient articulates with a provider.
8. Program standards will include the use of consumer satisfaction criteria as well as measures that assure access and efficiency at all stages of care.
9. The enterprise will have a mechanism for patient and provider articulation in areas where the enterprise does not provide a service level that is appropriate for care. These relationships will be defined and organized in a formal transfer agreement and under a transfer protocol that includes medical transport.
10. Leadership and administrative functions, medical and nonmedical, will be defined by written job descriptions, and there will be a recordkeeping function that records effort on both a time and a function basis.

---

* For the purposes of simplicity, I have labeled the organization that is the result of the physician-hospital integration as the enterprise. Call it what you will, these principles have to be in some form defined that is central to the planning function.

Some of these are challenging, but that does not mean that the groups involved in the development process should not have an open discussion. As an example, from a patient or consumer perspective, a single event at a hospital with doctors involved might have a half dozen or more different registration points—outpatient (or the practice site), inpatient, radiologist, anesthesiologist, physical therapy, discharge pharmacy, and home care or DME.* If the same information for the patient is required at each stop, couldn't there somehow be a common registration? If not, why not? Disneyland and most hotels allow a person to register once and then use a card or that single registration for the entire stay. Why can't this be something that could be implemented in most health care organizations? In any case, this is just one example of taking one of the principles and making a clear statement that there is a specific direction in which the health care partnership is headed.

If there are no core principals or standards, the individual physicians coming in to the process will assume that everything will be the same—if it were to be, why would anyone think it has value? A general understanding or a descriptive statement that references coordination or linkages will not foster consensus at a level where things can actually start to happen.

There has to be at least a general understanding and consensus on where the organization is headed and how the physician practices fit. The doctors have to buy in to the overall objectives, and their contracts have to be designed to be supportive of these goals. If there are no ideals stated or if they are vague, then the construction of the actual delivery system will be unfocused and the biggest force impacting any progress will be inertia. Being nonspecific or having a general idea that the parties will work together will allow contracts to be signed in the short term, but when there is a need to move forward as a unit, the organization will be faced with internal strife at the partnership level and disagreement within its own contracted physician workforce.

Choose a Structure That Fits the Situation

One often thinks of a project or a program in phases—immediate, near term, and long term. The challenge that health systems have is that they do not really have a capability to judge the nature of the long-term business environment. Since the passing of the Patient Protection and Affordable Care Act (PPACA), there have been numerous attempts to redefine and revoke the legislation. There have been modifications by the current administration to revise its own legislated programming. Many in Congress admit to not having even read the bill, and the final regulations are in constant flux. Planning and planners have to have a reference against some factors that can be used as anchors for discussion, and even

* DME—durable medical equipment.

though there may be contention over the near-term and long-term future of health care reimbursement, there are some assumptions that can be made for planning.

Whatever the form planning might take, it is safe to assume that (1) cost containment pressures will continue from every payer angle, (2) consolidation will continue to occur in every facet of health care, (3) health care provision will become even more capital-intensive and technologically focused, and (4) consumerism will emerge as a force. The idea of planning is not to question the forces that are evident, but to guess at the velocity and direction of change. There is obviously a need to restructure; the challenge is to form some bond in the health care system that can include practitioners in a structure that is feasible and flexible. Many alternative structures are in place. Table 11.1 reflects on their characteristics.

Advantages? Disadvantages? The options are pretty clear and, in the emerging health care marketplace, are becoming more so all the time (see Table 11.2).

Physicians Involved in the Care Process Must Have a Meaningful Role in Governance

All of the vision statements and planning processes and meetings to develop them will be wasted time and effort if there is not a key role for the practicing physicians in the governance of the enterprise. This means that the doctors who are in the direct provider status must be contributing to the overall governance at a level that allows them to have a dialogue about how their own arena is managed and how the operational decisions are made. Mistakes fall into a couple of general areas when governance is developed in organizations that define how doctors are organized and how physician resources are managed. Doctors are included, but the ones who are chosen are not practitioners, or the doctors who are chosen are practitioners but have not earned the respect of the other physicians in the group. Choice of the participants is as important as the choice of the overall governance model.

One last point about governance is that this is an elusive idea that is lost in parliamentary process.* In most dialogues with physicians, the planning process must be one that is participatory and decisions made by consensus. The physicians have been trained as scientists and have become businesspersons by necessity. They respond to a reasoned argument that is well defined and well documented. They also discern between true governance and the illusion of governance. It may seem like a trite statement, but if the right physicians are at the table with the right information, the final decisions are almost always correct.

What does it mean to have a meaningful role vs. just a seat at the table? It means that the governing body deals with important issues to the doctors, and that these

---

* For reference to parliamentary process, one usually looks to *Robert's Rules of Order*, in its 11th edition (first published in 1876), which is used as a guide by a person in a meeting that is labeled the sergeant at arms to keep the meeting moving and general order.

Table 11.1 Reorganization Characteristics

Maintain independent medical staff	Absolute physician autonomy	The physicians and the hospital maintain a traditional structure of market coexistence.
Address income issues only	Low system risk and cost	The hospital/system develops short-term strategies to address income support issues for physicians on a group-by-group basis.
Develop joint management entity		The physicians and the hospital/system develop a management company that has joint ownership and equity with potential profits and losses split. The entity acquires some of the professional corporation's assets.
Sale leaseback		The practice sells all actual assets to the system and leases them back for a specified (and controlled) sum. This could be fixed or it could be a percentage of gross.
Management services organization (MSO) unique to PC—split net		The system acquires assets from the PC, along with personnel and management. These are used to start a management services organization that has the PC as its primary customer.
MSO open to all—split net		The system develops an MSO that acquires assets initially from the physician group and which provides services to it and many other medical offices.
MSO/vendor group	High system risk and cost	The open MSO is formed, but the concept includes the opportunity for the management group to broker services between providers and reward efficiencies. The MSO/vendor becomes both a contractor of and subcontracted by the physician PC.
System purchases the PC	No physician autonomy	The system purchases the PC and the physicians accept contracts for their services with salaries and bonuses related to market externalities.

Table 11.2 Reorganization Implications (Governance)

Maintain independence	High autonomy. Low politics.	No relief for physician concerns. PC may lack potential for growth. System may lose market share as PC continues to weaken.
Address income issues only	Low political implications. Immediate and specific relief for some of the major physician concerns.	No long-term joint planning. No recognition of joint risk or development of efficiencies. Some implication that supports may have to extend to others.
Develop joint management entity	Physicians will develop a sense of participation in the entity and the management.	Physician equity is necessary. Physician time is necessary for addressing management and administrative issues.
Sale leaseback	Physicians divest capital assets, shifting risk.	No involvement or support in physician reimbursement or management. Potential exposure to market-based analysis, regarding inurement, etc.
MSO unique to PC—split net	Discretion is preserved between the groups.	Complex political problems with exclusivity. No economies of size or scale.
MSO open to all—split net	Less complex contractual relationship. Removes physician from some reimbursement or market exposure.	No involvement in contracting or efficiencies.

(Continued)

Table 11.2 Reorganization Implications (Governance) (Continued)

MSO/vendor group	Potential to gain economies of scale or size immediately. Opportunity for management and staff career ladder.	Some loss of uniqueness or autonomy for the PC. Increases the functional complexity.
System purchases PC	Physicians negotiate directly with the system for wage and salary support. Minimal physician environmental risk. Physicians absolutely minimize any administrative time.	Absolute loss of autonomy for the doctors. Capital-intensive. Politically dangerous.

issues are open for a variety of solutions without having the final solution channeled by the hospital. The best result, short term, may be to have the physicians agree to act in unison and to define a specific behavior that they can all get behind. Once there is consensus on how that decision can be made to be universal and the benefits of the common action can be studied, then the action or decision can be reconsidered to more fully advantage the hospital. By that time, hopefully, the hospital will have learned what standards are being applied in the selection of the referral partner.

Many times, the issues are obscured by meetings that are just badly planned and even more poorly executed. The meetings are ad hoc and unscheduled, crisis related and unscripted. The format of the meetings is generally defined by one issue or by one problem. There is no ability for consensus to develop because whoever called the session has the advantage of timing and information over the other party. Both doctors and hospital managers are frequently guilty of this type of miscommunication, and there is a way to avoid it. Meetings related to governance and oversight have to operate by an agreed set of rules:

Meetings related to governance issues or operational determinations have to be scheduled in advance. The only meetings that are not would be related to emergencies like peak loading problems or surprise accreditation inspections.

Meetings always have agendas distributed in advance, with the meeting only addressing issues included in the agenda. No added topics—no "new business" unless it is purely for information.

Agendas and minutes are issues driven and focused on decisions made, actions taken, issues to be considered, and the need for action. The minutes are not storybooks about who said what and who voted for whom. Any complex issue must have a white paper, a one-page descriptive text, that explains both sides of the issue.

Only elected representatives talk at a meeting. These are not town meetings—they are governance events that are meant to be supportive of goals and objectives and which need to be problem (and solution) oriented. Attendance can be allowed because the process should be transparent and open, but the determination made and the dialogue and background information have to be limited to principals involved in the final decision.

More will be offered about governance and meetings later in the text, especially as to how the governance process relates to budget issues and operations and management. The point in defining a way to meet in this space is to highlight the importance of changing a culture for both the hospital and the doctors. If the transaction does not mature into a collaborative governance format of some kind, then the only result will be a change in the financial underpinnings. True change, transformation, has to occur on all levels when organizations of different providers come together to serve patients from a new platform.

Physicians Must Be Allowed to Pursue Treatment Options in Line with Quality and Service Standards

The doctors have to be able to manage patients in a way that complements their practice style and experience levels. However, this process of patient management has to articulate with other functions that the health care enterprise has been created to fulfill. A physician's selection of a treatment option is based upon skill and experience. It might be based on ethnicity and where the doctors went to school. It might be based on who goes to which church or on a colleague's recommendation. It might be based on how easy it is for the front desk people to get referrals in to another office. Generally, the overall treatments and diagnostic processes can be measured against some norm, and they rarely are random. The choice of a referral for a specific problem is more difficult to manage and evaluate, but this is generally one core reason that the organization has been formed, and it is a chief concern of the sponsoring health care system. In order to know how to impact this process, the governance team must first understand where the referrals are being channeled and why.

The legal team will get squeamish when terms like *narrow network*, *steerage*, and *referral channeling* are used. They well should since this is an area of high legal sensitivity, and no one wants to have a deal or a transaction run afoul of any regulatory sanction against the redirection of patients for some kind of economic advantage. Nonetheless, referrals are made in an exam room and may be made on any number of professional and personal criteria. These might include standards of quality and care and communication that the physician has learned to respect over decades. The change of ownership and oversight may have been for the very reason of altering or impacting this decision; however, the contract probably clearly states that there is no implication that any part of the transaction relates to channeling referrals. This is a compliance issue, and one that is at odds with the nature of how and why networks are developed and maintained. They are all about the fact that referrals occur and each practice and physician exists within a network of their own design. The challenge for emerging health care systems is to understand the background behind that design and improve upon it. This cannot be done overnight, and it cannot be accomplished upon the execution of the agreement. The participants in the process must communicate openly on why a patient should be channeled in one direction over another and, when the reasons are understood for that process, install measures that ensure that the objectives behind the value-based network* are met.

One might consider imaging or lab services and note the many white boxes that are outside a typical primary care office. These are the ones that are similar to the old milk boxes that plied the roadways in the 1950s and 1960s when the milkman would actually deliver to the doorstep. Now, it is not milk and a delivery; the boxes are for lab samples and pickup. The doctors have little personal relationship with a pathologist, and generally the existence of these boxes has more to do with the payers and lab contracts than with physician choice of excellent lab support. In considering referrals to specialists and programs, the goal is to enhance the network that is linked to the system that is sponsoring the collaboration between the hospital and the doctor. If the system already has a great reputation and great doctors, this won't be a problem. But however great they may be, if they are unknown to the primary care practitioner, they may not be at the tip of the doctor's tongue when it is time to suggest a specialist.

This may cause friction when a physician transforms from private practice to one that is organized within a system of care. This is not much different than the traditional membership directories that have been published by managed care organizations for decades, and the doctor certainly is now using the facilities and equipment and the software that has been adopted for the enterprise, but traditional relationships are hard to define and harder to transform. As the medical system in the United States moves to an electronic medical record (EMR) and

* A value-based network is a network of hospitals and specialists that have been preselected by the sponsoring entity or a managed care organization or another entity on the basis of quality and price. Other factors that are emerging as indicators of choice are the measure of access and price transparency. Whether these are value measures is left to the reader to determine, but they are factors that are being used to define narrow networks of precontracted providers.

information about providers is more universally available, the referral choice may become almost as well defined as the protocols that are applied for care. At the early stages of development in any organization, this key reason for its existence is generally still left as something that is assumed.

Summary Issues

- Communication and governance are linked and neither will occur by accident. The doctors and the hospital have very different cultures for making decisions and implementation.
- Any new organization will require a new format for meetings and consensus development. Split votes among partners from different provider bases signal dissension, and this will eventually bring conflict.
- Core issues to any transaction and change in an organization always relate to referrals, no matter what the contracts imply. Because of regulatory issues and compliance factors, new models for how referrals are channeled will need to be developed.
- Probably the optics surrounding any reorganization will mean more than they should. This means that how communications and meetings are conducted will have an impact on the way that the parties interrelate and how committed they are to the process of change.

Chapter 12

Recognize the Different Parties to the Transaction

Administrators often use the term *physician* or *provider* or *medical staff* in a generic fashion when, in fact, there are all manner of providers, and each has differing background practice styles and personal goal sets. One must define the nature and style of the practice and the medical discipline and use a transaction that complements it. Just as a physician that owns a building will need a different approach than one that is renting, a physician specialty that has a number of ancillary services and support staff will be different from one that is focused on primary care. There are lots of potential types of transactions and many different types of practices and over 160 or so defined medical and physician areas of specialization. There are also many types of physician extenders and mid-level providers and specialty areas within each category.

Transactions result, however, in one common feature—some kind of service for hire that follows a transfer of an asset. This can mean direct employment or a service contract, but the components are pretty much the same for each.

What is the compensation for the services to be provided?
What services are going to be provided?
Is the contracted/employed party to be at risk?
What is the value of the asset or business entity transferred?

Beyond these simple factors, everything else is simply the detail that describes the relationship. Some may think that this is oversimplification, but an economist would point out that performance, pay, and risk are really the only three parameters to an employed or subcontracted relationship, and that employment and subcontracting are actually equivalent in nature, even if they differ legally.

The Result of the Transaction Can Often Mean More Than the Transaction Itself

The hospital or health system needs to have some basic idea of where it needs to go, or where it wants to go, before it begins to acquire physician practices and hire the doctors that go with them. Regrettably, the hospital generally finds itself in a situation of reacting to market forces that are pushing it beyond its planning horizon. These forces can be the actions of a competitor, the emergence of a new factor or channel of health care delivery in the local marketplace, new programs sponsored by the payer community, reimbursement changes or structural payment program changes (like the Patient Protection and Affordable Care Act (PPACA)), or simply pressure from individual physician groups. Probably, for most hospitals, all of these factors have something to do with why they are out purchasing practices.

In simple terms, if there is a plan, it probably includes hiring providers, and if there is not a plan, the hospital is probably hiring providers as a reactive measure to something it fears. The doctors are also approaching transactions out of fear of an unknown future, and this combination can make for badly constructed and executed deals. The institution is generally ill-equipped to manage a physician practice, and this is not because they are bad managers; it is simply that they do not manage this style business and their experience base and technology and infrastructure are not suited for the task of managing individual units of professionals that have an entrepreneurial orientation and no taste whatsoever for an organizational style of management.

The transactions themselves are easy. The vision of where the organization wants to go is generally not very clear, nor has it been defined well for its administrative team.* The process of negotiating a deal and executing the transaction is a process, the steps of which can be defined. The transition from community hospital and private practice to consolidated and integrated enterprise is a journey that is uncharted and for which the travelers are unprepared. One author, writing about the general state of affairs between providers and hospitals, put it this way, "The mutual interdependency of hospitals and doctors has long been a source of

* The appendix includes a sample policy statement that outlines an approach to practice acquisitions. Few boards or institutions have actually implemented such a policy or have any kind of organized approach to purchasing and incorporating a physician practice within their service lines.

angst that has resulted in continually evolving roles and adaption."* This will seem like an understatement to most hospital administrators who are going through the reorganization of their traditional medical staff and reforming them into a cadre of employed and contracted physicians.

This transition is not only related to the practicing physician who accompanies his or her practice from privately owned status to part of a hospital system. There are also doctors who have never been in, and never want to be in, private practice. They are emerging from training with considerable debt and with a need for security and salary to be able to pay off that debt. They are not in a financial position, nor do they have a mind-set that allows them to consider, to buy in to or start a practice. They will go into the jobs that are being created by hospitals that are transforming their medical staff from private attending practitioners to hired and contracted providers, and they will go there with no understanding and without any experience gained from senior mentor physicians who can groom them for traditional patient service in a private practice environment.

Some will say that hiring the uninitiated practitioner who has never been in private practice is an easier task than forming a relationship with a former practice owner. This may be true in some respects, but the models that are being used to transition private practitioners into an integrated medical staff are being shaped and constructed for private practicing doctors, and they emulate a model that the hospital is generally trying to abandon. Bringing the new hires into contract models meant to attract doctors from an older system of care—fee for service—may be adding an extra layer of complexity that is not necessary and which may further inhibit changes that need to be made in the future as payment systems move more toward payment for quality measures and care coordination.

It Is Important to Understand Differing Perspectives

There are some groups of doctors that already are contracted to hospitals or who are aligned with hospitals for reasons not related to their typical medical staff membership functions. Some doctor groups may never really be part of any kind of alignment,† and some may be outside the reach of health systems altogether. Table 12.1 details the different types of practices and disciplines that must be considered in the new health care enterprise. It is repeated from Chapter 4 in order to reflect which specialities might be changing in the near term.

* Margaret F. Schulte, *Healthcare Delivery in the U.S.A.*, CRC Press, Taylor & Francis Group, New York, 2009, p. 83.

† Retail medical services such as those being deployed by Walgreens, CVS, and others may be outside the immediate scope of health care systems, at least in the immediate and near term.

Table 12.1 Same General Categories—New Challenges

Hospital-based and hospital-dependent practices *These groups now may be national or regional groups with extensive political and functional clout and with relationships that extend well beyond their departmental service.*	Emergency room physician Anesthesiologists Radiologists Pathologists Intensivists Hospitalists
Capital-intensive and independent *These are groups that now have access to capital from private equity markets and managed care plans.*	Ophthalmologists Plastic surgeons Orthopods
Capital-intensive and dependent *Private equity may have also allowed these doctors to be independent of the hospital.*	Cardiologists Nephrologists Obstetricians Urologists Oncologists
Non-capital-intensive specialty *Many options exist for doctors in specialities where they can collaborate with their peers, going directly to payers.*	General surgeons Dermatologist Internal medicine (pulmonology, GI)
Primary care *This is a speciality that is being redefined by retail medicine and urgent care center access and employer based clinics.*	Family practice Internal medicine Pediatrics

These categories will be dealt with in subsequent chapters, but the point here is to make a distinction. The anesthesia practice* is generally one that is organized in the local marketplace in a very different fashion from a pediatric practice. One size does not fit all, but there can be a common approach to one discipline, like

* Actually, there may be another entire category that cannot fit on a chart of this nature, and that is the practice that is part of a national or regional enterprise. Super practices emerged in the 1980s as corporations began to purchase practice assets and align them within a physician practice management corporation (PPMC). This model failed, but there is a new model emerging that consolidates large specialty practices such as anesthesia and radiology. Dealing with these organizations is often a different challenge than dealing with a group that is specific to any one hospital or health system since they have an independent management focus and the physicians may be shareholders or contract employees that are not responsive to local trends.

community-based primary care, that is consistent, while there is a totally different approach to practices that are using "heavy equipment" and those which are "bed dependent."

Are There Any Universal Truths?

Actually, there are. Just as the expectations and responsibilities of a health care system can be generalized, hospitals need to have doctors address key areas that are complementary. These should be in every arrangement:

Coverage of the emergency department (especially with respect to EMTALA*)
Coverage of any clinical access for Medicaid and self-pay (uninsured) patients
Coverage of clinical teaching responsibilities
Support for health system-sponsored outreach initiatives
Support for health system recruiting initiatives
Assurance of coverage for system-approved managed care contracts
Support of community service commitments
Inpatient coverage for code cases and intensive care units
Coverage of employee health matters (the employees of the health system)
Active support for accreditation processes and licensure activities

There are probably a host of other requirements depending upon the hospital and health system, and besides the basics listed above, there are some contract issues that can be very desirable to a health care system. These would include commitments to assist with planning and marketing of hospital programs, and they might also include assisting the enterprise in defining its service complement and in assuring that capital that is dedicated to the activity will be more secure. These are "code words" for the following contract components:

Some definition of exclusivity or primacy of service
An assurance of a restrictive covenant or noncompete guarantee
A commitment to a span of geographic presence
Continuing support for the original, or contracted, range of services
Participation with product line development
A commitment to use system-sponsored ancillaries
Participation in data exchange programs
Participation in universal registration and reporting functions
Participation with joint promotional activities

---

* Emergency Medical and Active Labor Act (1986), http://www.cms.gov/Regulations-and-Guidance/Legislation/EMTALA/index.html?redirect=/emtala/.

The point in making lists of this nature is to assure that nothing gets lost or forgotten as the parties craft whatever arrangement they embark upon. Direct contracting in this case is different than direct employment. In the employment model, the employed provider commits to the goals and objectives of the employer. In the contracting model, the support and joint participation in any program activity must be spelled out. However, in a contract that simply states "all time and all effort," there may be some confusion about what that actually means. Specificity at the outset of the contracting process will always produce a better partnership.

When hospitals or health systems define contractual relationships, they are definitely not contracting from a position of weakness. There is a corresponding list of items that they can control, not all of which might be obvious. They definitely have trade and brand recognition. They control access to procedural units. They can channel referrals from a variety of resources, and they can deploy resources to support programs that might be patient or consumer specific. In the case of technology, they have linkages that are important to everything from registration to the electronic medical record (EMR) to ancillaries. Often, the access to staff support or inclusion in a medical office building or the granting of different levels of privileges can be a factor in the way that a physician group aligns with a hospital. There is also the implied threat that the hospital will develop a network or something like an ACO[*] and leave out specific doctors.

In forming relationships, subtleties count. Practice access to information and referrals is also critical. A surgical practice that is not on the emergency department (ED) rotation listing or which does not get support from house officers is less effective and efficient than one that does. Like Congress or the Senate, the placement of a key physician from a practice on an important committee can raise the practice image, and it certainly allows the practice and the doctors within it to have a better idea of what is going on within the institution. The point is that hospitals have contract terms and what might be described as a variety of noncontract benefits, which, if you are from the old school, might be referred to as "green stamps," which are nonfinancial benefits that have definite long-term economic impact.

Transition Is More Than a Corporate Function—It Is a Cultural Reprogramming

Doctors come from a different world than hospital management. They are trained differently, and they contract from a different perspective. If the doctor is a private practitioner, he or she has relocated specifically to an area or region and has invested

[*] Accountable care organization. This is a form of an organization often referenced as it relates to the PPACA as one that coordinates care for a large group of patients. Interestingly, a group of physicians could form an ACO without a hospital but not without significant capital. The hospital, however, cannot form an ACO without a physician base.

in his or her group or practice. If he or she has been in an area for any length of time, he or she may have witnessed changes in administrative staff at the hospital and might have seen actual hospital closures and mergers. He or she has certainly experienced changes in reimbursement and is now facing an uncertain future under the PPACA.

Hospitals need to have flexibility. Many hospitals purchased practices in the past, and there are many references in the hospital literature regarding the cost of physician practices and the ongoing cost of maintaining them. "The last time we tried this, providing tacit incentives for hospitals to roll up doctors in the 1990s, it ended badly. The hospitals and practice management companies that went on buying binges—scooping up independent medical practices—mostly failed. The doctors unwound the relationships, and went back to running their own offices."*

Table 12.2 details the differing perspectives of doctors and hospitals regarding general contract terms.

Hospital management may also want involvement in committees, the ability to assign a doctor in multiples settings, and minimum production quotas. The doctors may wish for protection of practice franchises, longer-term (evergreen-style†) contracts, and extensive benefits. Discussions will include the issue of additional pay for "extra" work and the concept of signing bonuses. New physicians may require assistance with the repayment of loans or assistance in housing and the relocation of spouses and families.

The Future of Independent Hospitals and Private Practice Is Limited

What options are available to the private practitioner? What alternatives are available? Often, it is helpful to reflect on realistic alternatives as the contracting process takes form. Many of the issues are evident and the alternatives seem limitless, but they really reduce to maintaining independence or linking with another practice or health care system. Each has its drawbacks and advantages, but few practitioners really analyze them in a formal fashion. This is pretty much the case with hospitals and their reaction to the marketplace and to the practice acquisition opportunities that they have. Little planning followed by precipitous behavior results in a transition process that can be calamitous.

---

* Scott Gottlieb, MD, writing in *Forbes* and in the *Wall Street Journal*, http://www.forbes.com/sites/scottgottlieb/2013/03/15/hospitals-are-going-on-a-doctor-buying-binge-and-it-is-likely-to-end-badly/.

† An evergreen contract is one that renews periodically without review or termination. This type of contract is not allowed by health care counsel under compliance guidelines as they are presently published and generally understood. However, this does not prevent doctors from seeking these terms and from hospitals constructing contracts that approach them.

Table 12.2 Contracts—Different Perspectives

Component	*Hospital Perspective*	*Physician Perspective*
Term	Shorter	Long, with a variety of outs
Renewal	Silent	Guaranteed, initial standard is 1 year (maybe 2)
Termination	Longer requirements for employee (6 months?); without cause or cause defined by employer	Restrict to egregious events and defined occurrences (loss of license, malpractice, conviction on a felony, loss of privileges, etc.)
Salary	Fixed or subject to collections or practice productivity	Internally consistent and consistent with the local marketplace
Increases	Silent	Specified as an annual increase to correspond to fixed percentage or the consumer price index, whichever is greater
Bonus	Silent or to be determined, group driven and related to profit or revenue	Specific, individual, and performance driven, independent of collections or profits
Medical staff privileges (especially in hospital-based physician groups)	Privileges required but co-terminal with the contract	No reference to hospital privileges; due process preserved
Benefits	Employee contribution	Employer provided
Malpractice	Owned by employer and limited to actual purpose of employment	Unlimited application with guarantee of continuation and "tail" coverage*

* Continuing coverage for acts of malpractice committed during the term of the contract. This is coverage for prior occurances that may have been discovered later in the physician's career, when he or she is in another job situation.

(Continued)

Table 12.2 Contracts—Different Perspectives (Continued)

Component	*Hospital Perspective*	*Physician Perspective*
Hourly and functional commitment	Undefined; all time, all efforts	Specified hours and shifts and the ability to apply effort in other functional activities
Paid time off	Sick days, continuing medical education (CME), vacation, personal days, bereavement days, defined and specified	Number of days—any purpose without definition
Noncompete	Yes, including liquidated damages and specifying both a restrictive covenant and noncompetition clause; often including nonsolicitation language regarding patients and employees	None
Call coverage	To be determined, generally commensurate with others of the same class or position	Fixed and predictable, subject to review and comparison with other specialties or national norms

However, maintaining the status quo in the face of changing markets and reimbursement has its own potentially disastrous results. The one thing that is a slight advantage is that maintaining independence is an option that might offer some flexibility where aligning with a health care organization is often a choice that cannot be easily reversed.* Frankly, a similar statement can be made for a hospital. The traditional community-based hospital has a medical staff that is changing one transaction and one contract at a time.

* Some contracts provide for an "unwind" where the practice is allowed to retreat from the arrangement as long as it allows the health care system to recover any investments. However, the reality is that the practice can seldom obtain the capital necessary to achieve this sort of rollback. In the 1990s, when there were practices being "taken back" by doctors, there was a more forgiving compliance environment.

Summary Issues

- One size does not fit all. Doctors are different, and each category of physician may require different approaches and a variety of structures even though some contract goals may span many models.
- Hospitals rarely plan for practice acquisitions, and therefore they cannot predict accurately any results. At some point in time the institution has to choose a central theme and some basic goals and define a process of management that is, hopefully, supported by the physician contracting process.
- Not all opportunities for integration make sense. Not all partners in the health care spectrum have goals that can be consistent with those of a hospital. The health care organization should be shopping for components of a health care delivery system and not acting as a pawn shop for unwanted or worn-out practices.

Chapter 13

Address Issues of Colleagues, Culture, and Politics

A practice is part of the whole organized approach to the emerging marketplace, and the physician is part of the practice. But the entire enterprise has to exist as a part of something that can actually contract with managed care organizations and with things that are in place, being developed and being conceived under organizations that will use tools like accountable care organizations (ACOs) and insurance exchanges. These are taking forms that are not unlike the subcapitated contracts that most institutions played with in decades past. What is the same seems obvious; what is different is that the physicians are mostly "in-house," and there are better management systems in the provider environment.

Physicians and Providers in Alternative Organizations—the IPA and PHO Revisited

No matter what it is called, not every physician may be in the "hired model" or fully integrated. Some may still maintain independence, and some may work with other organizations that are not only not collaborative, but competing. Few health systems will have the capital and the energy to fully integrate the entire spectrum of services necessary to serve an ACO population or a managed care cohort of some kind.

The organizations may still need to have a business model that includes some kind of physician organization. If it does, it needs to do it carefully and under a plan that has some basic guidelines outlining what it is supposed to do and how its members are to be involved and incorporated within the services design. Although the following points are generic, they should be a starting point for discussion in any planning process that includes a variety of doctors in a range of contracted models. The managed care companies are organized, ACOs are organized, and the doctors who contract with them need some kind of organization. If they cannot all be in one group and under one billing number and management structure, maybe they need to be in an organization that emulates that model.

Some goals for an initial planning session might include:

- To utilize group behavior and collaboration to assure a high quality of patient service as measured by national outcome standards and customer satisfaction
- To assist all members in achieving contract standards that are prevalent in the local market area in a form that reflects a fee schedule and remuneration program that is competitive externally and recognizes internal membership contributions
- To operate an efficient and businesslike service that brings top management talent to directly support efficient and effective medical professionals and practices
- To impact the system in a manner that will allow a true partnership between doctors, patients, providers, and payers in order to foster a true understanding of the value of health, instead of merely the cost of health services
- To use the independent provider association (IPA) (physician-hospital organization (PHO) or management services organization (MSO)) group power and the synergy between independent physicians, contracted practices, management, capital, and the critical mass of patients to produce a working model that will have significant market impact and a healthy bottom line
- To develop an entity that will be able to coordinate the activities of its member physicians with the supportive efforts of the health care system in cooperation with its array of contracted and employed physicians and its ancillary support units
- To develop an entity that will have the required breadth and depth to accept responsibility for populations under a variety of scenarios and contracting methodologies
- To develop a structure that will foster the input of physicians into the governing process of the joint venture and which will command the respect of managed care programs, partner institutions, and subscribing physicians
- To develop systems and support mechanisms to allow member physicians and related entities to participate in competitive contracting initiatives,

case management, patient-based management programs, quality assurance programs, total quality management (TQM), utilization review processes, claims processing, etc.

- To participate in the development of an integrated health care system that can provide a full spectrum of service from initial diagnosis to treatment and discharge, including follow-up rehabilitative care, long-term care, and subacute care services when indicated

These goals are somewhat lofty, but the organized planning process has to start with something other than a blank piece of paper and the idea that the past practices and practice elements are going to be easily transformed into a structure that can deal with the realities of the new environment.

Medical Staff Issues and Trends—The Structure of the New Medical Staff

The traditional medical staff was comprised of voluntary physicians in the community electing to join a hospital staff and simply following some credentialing rules and attending an occasional medical staff meeting. Staying current on a medical staff meant keeping patient records up to date and maintaining a set of professional credentials. The hospital took a rather passive role, but eventually most hospitals realized that the marketplace and the competition for inpatients required an active role in shaping the medical staff to assure access and to develop programming. Recruitment at the hospital level matched the recruitment processes that doctors were doing in their own individual practices to assure secession and to gain some kind of value for the equity in the practices as they were sold from one generation of physicians to the next.

This is all different with the changing health care reimbursement structure and the organized marketplaces that have formed around it. There is little, if any, goodwill in a private practice, and if there is goodwill, there is no real market in which it can be sold. The hospital recruiting process is an active part of both community planning and the need to complement expensive and expansive institutional programming with the talent to run the machinery of health care delivery. Also, there are now any number of other nonhospital environments that are emerging where providers and practitioners meet patients and serve them in nontraditional settings. A "medical staff development plan" is generally the tool that is used to define how a hospital might channel its physician recruiting resources.

What Defines a Good Plan?

1. A comprehensive report that serves to confirm, identify, or propose alternatives to the client's strategic direction relative to the its primary care base and select specialties. Understanding that the primary objective of the project is to strengthen overall hospital volumes, we will evaluate all relevant clinical services and geographic market areas.
2. Current specialty-specific supply counts and projections for future needs as defined by objective market data compared to industry-accepted benchmarks for physician supply per 100,000 lives (including age- and sex-adjusted population and specialty-specific visit standards).
3. Current and future adequacies/gaps in physician supply relative to existing strategic direction and market development goals as identified by hospital leadership.
4. Stakeholder-reviewed and -endorsed recommendations for affiliation, recruitment, retention, and long-term provider success, including strategies and tactics for graduating primary care residents, senior physicians approaching retirement, employed physicians, physicians with divided loyalties, and physicians currently practicing at competing institutions.
5. Identification and evaluation of realistic legal structures and financial strategies that could be employed to enhance utilization of specialty services by nonaffiliated primary care physicians, recruit physicians to fill identified community and institutional gaps, and strengthen partnerships with physicians/groups through mutual benefit and unity of purpose.

Medical staff development is a concept usually associated with hospitals and medical centers that value the doctors on the staff as the "distribution arm" for hospital products and services. The cultivation of a strong and loyal medical staff is recognized as a key to the survival of the hospital as a viable economic entity. However, the emphasis is now shifting to approaches that quantify each component of the medical staff to rank their impact and value. The answer is no longer a simple "more is better." The new question is: Which departments or doctors might make the most substantial contribution relative to any attainment cost?

Medical staff development for the group practice is even more important than it is for a hospital since the size and composition of the group are directly related to revenue development. The preservation of product lines, key segments of the patient base, and even entire departments might be related to one or two key physicians. Mortality and morbidity risk is more pronounced because a group usually has a less diverse base than that of a hospital, yet group practices seldom have a formal planning process for the preservation, enhancement, and improvement of their key component resource—the doctor. This chapter attempts to outline the key factors in the planning process and indicators that might be referenced by the physicians as they initiate this process.

A medical staff development plan should be structured to assure the *continuation of the present service level* to the community.

Replacements for doctors approaching retirement age or anticipating a marked reduction in contribution levels should be recruited.

Existing departments, franchises, patient groups, or areas that are underserved should be staffed.

A medical staff development plan should develop business from presently controlled patient bases.

Referrals to outside subspecialists should be quantified, and when absolute numbers indicate feasibility, the subspecialty should be internalized by the group.

Referrals lost due to geographic or institutional issues should be quantified, and when feasible, liaisons with groups or doctors represented in those areas or entities should be formalized.

Consults by hospital-based physicians or doctors who are aligned with procedural or diagnostic units not owned by the group should be studied, and when appropriate, the business should be converted to fall under group control.

A medical staff development plan should address perceived needs of the physician group members relative to *quality of care or quality of practice.*

Physician members should be polled to determine their perception of need for backup, quality controls, coverage, accessibility, coordination, patient continuity, service levels, etc. Where there is a consensus, the board should consider recruiting to fill these perceived needs.

Internal utilization studies, cross-referral patterns, quality and efficiency reviews, etc., should be analyzed. Where deficiencies occur that negatively affect the group and its patients, or which undermine the overall mission, there may be indication for board action that results in recruiting.

A medical staff development plan should anticipate market opportunities and address the competitive nature of the health care catchment area.

An analysis of need in the community should be conducted to highlight product lines, geographic locations, services, etc., that represent targets of business or service opportunity for the group. If practical, after risk and investment have been considered, the group should address these needs through the medical staff development process.

Referral patterns to subspecialties external to the market area should be analyzed to assess the feasibility of *local* provision of care as an improved service.

Competitors should be routinely studied to determine opportunities for improved competitive positions, collaboration, or acquisition. Special notice should be taken of those practices that might be anticipating change themselves.

A medical staff development plan should accommodate liaisons, affiliations, collaborative ventures, and joint ventures. It should support referral arrangements with other entities and physician groups.

Referral patterns into the group from external practices should be identified and quantified. There should be a component of the plan that supports and enhances these practitioners.

Opportunities for cooperation with other noncompetitive entities should be identified and pursued. The board may pursue formal (or informal) relationships developed with supportive providers in addition to, or in lieu of, direct recruiting.

A medical staff development plan is the product of a process that is both qualitative and quantitative. There are basic financial aspects involved as well as philosophical and social implications. An effective plan is a diagram for strategic action and a program that should improve the income and equity position of each corporate member.

Summary Issues

- Medical staff planning is outmoded and old school. Organizations should be doing population management planning. This means that first and foremost, there has to be a population to manage.
- Old adages and impressions will no longer work. It might be better to have a fresh start with a new physician than to try to convert a traditionalist to new practice patterns.
- Most investments in medical staff formation and transformation will not yield a return in the near term—maybe not for 5 years. The system has to have the staying power to make it to the end game.

Chapter 14

Discern between Patient Management and Practice Management

The type of a structure that manages a hospital or health system has a form equivalent to the nature and scope of the institution. Seldom is this "sized" to accommodate a private practice. Transition comes from a variety of departments and may be a process that is not only far reaching, but also overreaching. An example is often evident in purchasing. The private practice may have an account at Costco™* that it has used for office supplies and the hospital buys through a buying group (group purchasing organization (GPO)). The Costco pricing may be cheaper on some items than what the hospital has been able to achieve in its professionally staffed purchasing function. Also, Costco acts as an inventory support function for the private office. It always has a stock of whatever is needed. If a practice runs out of something, there is always a trip to Costco. This keeps inventory low, and logic would dictate that the practice would buy from the most cost-effective source. This may not fit the process as it is managed in a health system that has very precise and, maybe, automated purchasing function that is linked to bookkeeping and accounting functions. Not only is the process changed, but there is now a need to warehouse supplies, and there may be increased supply costs.

* Costco Wholesale is a national chain that provides wholesale pricing to individuals on a membership basis. Arguably, it is comparable to chains like Walmart and Sam's Club for prices on a variety of consumer and business goods.

In the end, the purchasing is going to be done through the hospital. This doesn't mean that the practice was badly managed. It just means that the hospital has a structure to which the practice must now adhere. The change is directed by the need for the hospital to be internally consistent and consider pricing and inventory control differently than a practice might.

The purchasing example may seem trite, but it is the type of thing that can be an irritant because the changes may be irrelevant to the practitioner, and they may actually be counterintuitive. A better example and one that is generally positive is the human resources function. Practices may be more casual about HR than a hospital, and the processes that a hospital uses for hiring and promoting staff and managing employees often will produce a more stable and better-trained and qualified workforce. This also may be at a cost, but the benefits may be more apparent than the doctor's experience with the purchasing department.

Accounting, billing, coding, purchasing, facilities, grounds keeping, housekeeping, maintenance, IT, HR, and a variety of other health systems have to be included in a transition. Generally, the challenge is to coordinate their efforts and to have a single person that can act as a traffic cop to assure that the practice continues to operate and serve patients while the mechanics of practice business transformation is occurring. This person must have the trust of both the physicians and providers in the practice as well as the hospital. Moreover, within the hospital environment, he or she must have some level of authority to cross departmental lines and act as a buffer between the bureaucratic processes of the institution and the relatively flat structure of management that characterizes most professional practices.

What Is the Commitment Level to a Different Level and Style of Governance?

Physicians are trained to be in charge, and hospitals and health systems have a similar imperative to lead rather than follow. The health system is committed to community service and self-preservation, and the physician is committed to the patient care and personal security. If we break this down further, each is also committed to minimizing risk and continued growth of some kind. The doctors control their own environment in the exam room, and if they are a business owner, they also control the environment in which they practice. That is, if their practice is of a modest size, they have more involvement in the governance of the practice and in controlling the administrative functions as well as patient care.

It is instructive to look at organizations that are formed by providers and note that they are labeled independent provider associations (IPAs), and there is not the use of terms like *organization* or *co-op* or *collaborative*. The doctors want to have just enough coordination to be able to control their place in the market without giving up control of their practices. Many IPAs and physician-hospital organizations

(PHOs) cling to the idea that they are organizations that are comprised of independent businesses rather than consolidated entities. However, most realize that they are in a market that is being controlled by payers and other organized entities, and that there is a cost to independence. Examples of successful ventures are often used to describe how fiercely independent businesses thrive in a co-op model while maintaining strict autonomy. The farmer's grange and the craftsman's guild come to mind. These examples do not translate to medicine and the delivery of health care since they really reflect a group of homogeneous producers with very distinct and narrow products coming together to achieve control over direct costs or something like market entry. The health care field is too complex and has too many layers of interrelated product categories to be compared to these rather simple models.

As a physician practice grows from a solo practitioner model to the more complex group models, whether they are multispecialty or just a form of a larger single specialty group, the individual physician gives up a degree of control with each stage of growth. Simply stated, the larger the practice, the less impact a single doctor has in any individual decision. When the practice merges with another practice or when equity is reorganized in a joint venture or a transaction with a health care system, the individual doctor has little impact unless he or she is involved in the governance structure. He or she needs to look at his or her contract to see how his or her involvement is defined. In a practice of three or four doctors, the practice governing body is meeting any time the doctors get together in the break room for coffee. Bigger may be better, but it is not necessarily easier.

Hospitals have the same type of a challenge when linking with physicians in some formal fashion. Shared governance means less control and more consensus building. A hospital that relies upon its medical staff structure for the deployment of health care may have a relatively simple task in maintaining its governance as a pure board and administrative function, but it might be challenged when it has to go into the marketplace to contract under new forms of reimbursement. When it links up with a physician complement, hired or otherwise, it is exploring new communication challenges and new opportunities (and hazards) in untested governance models.

Operational Management Is Not Governance—Managers Manage and Doctors Govern

It is helpful to actually delve into the core definitions of administration, governance, and management when discussing operational matters within a medical practice environment. The doctor who has been in private practice has been in the position of doing it all for a period of years, and this brings some level of empowerment along with a high degree of satisfaction and comfort. If there were any level of confidence that this feeling could continue unchallenged by reimbursement or other business environment changes, no practice would ever be sold or transitioned to a hospital. The practitioner who is new to the field of medicine, never before in private practice, also has a sense of what a doctor should be and who should be in charge. This is instilled through a training structure that moves physicians through various levels of educational and apprenticeship levels that value structure and demonstrate levels of privilege that equate rewards to the level of control over any particular patient or general health care environment.

Actually, the doctor or provider can really manage very little except that in his or her own zone of direct control and oversight. Within the exam room, he or she is the preeminent expert and a diagnostician and overall conductor of the resources that relate to therapy of all kinds. Of course, his or her role is limited by established protocols, managed care companies, patient expectations, and resource availability. Outside the exam room and the direct control of patient care, he or she is in an environment controlled by regulation, social convention, accreditation standards, legal risk parameters, and a variety of institutional rules and regulations. Doctors and providers actually control very little in the direct operations of their practice when one considers the realm in which the practice has to operate as a business and the regulatory arena in which the doctor has to act.

It is more useful to have the doctors and their support personnel and the hospital recognize that there are differing levels of control and authority. Operational control and management are more oriented to the direct oversight of the work environment, patient flow, staffing, inventory management, coding, billing, and physician direct control functions. Medical management of a patient is confined by the determinations the doctor makes over the patient care and medical processing of a patient (like ordering lab tests and channeling referrals). The governance of the enterprise is where the determinations are made concerning how the overall structure of the organization will be formed and how it will relate to the environment and the market it serves.

Governance impacts the overall structure and makeup of the practice environment and its core values, while the management of the practice is related to the day-to-day operational issues, many of which are simply an oversight matter requiring very little decision-making background but a high degree of inspection (as opposed to analysis). An example is the routine payment of invoices for needed supplies or overhead items. This is an operational issue, and it has to be monitored and needs oversight and inspection to make sure that the process is well done and efficient, but the phone bill is going to be paid regardless. On the other hand, the replacement of a phone system for an office could run into tens of thousands of dollars, and even if it is indicated, the amount of the expenditure and the disruptive impact would require that it be discussed among practice principals. The challenge is not how to decide, but at what level each decision might be made. The following listing suggests some of the levels where these concepts can be best assigned.

Governance issues or decisions requiring significant consensus between principals:
- Practice relocation or significant reorganization
- Addition of a provider to the practice unit
- Change of practice infrastructure (electronic medical record (EMR), on-site diagnostic services, etc.)
- Participation (de-participation) in a managed care program
- Determination of general staffing patterns and office support patterns
- Significant changes in top-level management staff
- Counseling/disciplinary action or termination of a provider

Management issues or decisions in which the practitioner might not be directly involved:
- Changes in a supply vendor
- Changes in staff salaries and benefits
- Addition of a specific staff member (nonprovider)
- Replacement of a staff member
- Disciplinary action against a staff member
- Renegotiation of a lease, loan, or other agreement
- Authorization of routine payables
- Oversight of the AR function (write-offs, advancement to collections, etc.)
- Oversight of routine maintenance items, refurbishment of equipment, etc.

Practitioner decides—medical care:
- Diagnostic processes
- Treatment determination and medical prescriptions
- Referral decisions
- Patient information processes
- Need for patient follow-up

Obviously, these listings are not exhaustive, but they are meant to demonstrate that there are limits to what a doctor can actually decide even if he or she owns the practice. If he or she is a provider under a contract of some kind, there are limits to what the hospital or the health system can mandate. The process of defining these levels of decision making is also further defined by protocols that have been established by medical and contracting organizations and by contracts that have been developed between the providers and the health care system. These are further constrained by regulations and by compliance standards and risk management processes, all of which are in a state of constant change.

In a formal structure, it is helpful to think of what can be defined by contract vs. what can only be defined externally. Contract definition is required for overall provider schedules, call schedules, and changes in income determination. These are all pretty obvious. Working conditions and areas of professional latitude are often defined by the regulatory environment or by risk management strategies. The physician is in a constant state of discovering and defining what he or she perceives to be a narrowing range of self-determination, while the hospital is challenged by maintaining a business case in an environment where it is constantly hampered by doctors who define operational issues within a framework of quality care and patient need.

The process is also important. Table 14.1 describes one approach to keeping information moving in a way that physicians and staff can be assured of input. The process is simple: no decisions are made unless they are staffed* and on a posted agenda. The governance board operates off a published calendar.

Why the Resulting Product Is Often Less Than the Sum of the Parts

Hospitals add cost to practices, and the cost is generally not recovered by patient billings being improved† or by economies of scale. Generally, this is due to several factors, all of which have been well documented in a variety of ways over many projects and venues.

- The hospital spends a considerable amount of money on the transaction itself, almost none of which can be recaptured in cost reports and from cost reimbursement payers.
- The hospital system generally has better benefits (more costly benefits) than the local physician practices, and the transformation of the physician staff increases benefit costs for the practice.
- The hospital generally has more generous pay scales for its employees than the same practices when owned and managed by doctors.
- The physician practices are generally undercapitalized and need expensive upgrades for computer systems and EMRs and other links to registration and registry functions.
- Physician practices do not manage themselves, and the hospital needs to have additional management personnel assigned to the functions of managing the practice, if only to act as a liaison.
- Suppliers and contracts that have been negotiated by physicians may be renegotiated by supplier at a contract rate that is higher than the practice

* *Staffed* means that the decision has an administrative report and a formal recommendation.

† Some practice reorganizations result in the transfer of the billing base from a physician office environment to a hospital outpatient environment. The latter has a higher billing rate with Medicare and with managed care companies. This is an anomaly that may be different region to region and state to state, and it may be short-lived as more payers gravitate to universal pricing of outpatient services and components of care move to bundled pricing arrangements.

Table 14.1 A Governance Calendar

	Finance Committee	*Other Committees*	*Board*
January			
February	Review of year-end financials		
March			Review of year-end performance and authorization for tax submittals
April	Review of first quarter performance		
May		Medical director reports on hospital-related issues, staffing, PR, planning, etc.	
June			
July	Review of second quarter performance, performance at mid-year		
August	Prepare and submit budget for the upcoming calendar year		
September		Income determination subcommittee meets and addresses any outstanding issues	

(Continued)

Table 14.1 A Governance Calendar (Continued)

	Finance Committee	*Other Committees*	*Board*
October	Review of third quarter performance and first 9 months		Approve budget for the upcoming calendar year
November		Executive committee review of CEO performance	
December			

historically pays. Simply put, hospitals pay more than physician practices for some services.

- The credentialing and licensing and organizational costs of a hospital-run practice are generally higher. For example, a physician practice may have a simple and straightforward approach to employee hiring, and a hospital may have a process that requires background checks and drug testing. Certain positions in a physician practice may be covered by a medical assistant (MA), and a hospital system may have a policy that a registered nurse needs to be in an ambulatory environment.
- Physician owners have salary structures that take advantage of the tax breaks that inure to business owners, and they may not recognize costs that are inherent in a standard business operation. When they move to employed status in a hospital, additional contract features like medical education costs, vacation days, and other benefits that were implied in the private practice are converted to some kind of defined benefit with associated costs.
- Hospitals assign overhead factors to budgeting within departments and across projects. These are costs that an independent practice would not have allocated.

All of these factors will combine to add a considerable factor ($50,000 or more) annually to the cost of doing business when a practice is acquired. This is all part of the investment. This is not a reason to avoid the incorporation of the practice within the health care system; it is a reason to do so carefully and within a process that has an overall financial plan that is realistic.

Summary Issues

- Practice management is different when done by a hospital or a health system. It is neither better nor worse—just different. This differing approach must be part of the management process.
- Health systems have to plan for added costs when a practice is incorporated into the health care structure. The costs can be recognized and predicted, but seldom will economies of scale offset them.
- Doctors and hospitals under any process should discuss management and governance in detail, agreeing upon who can decide on which issues. Generally speaking, the doctor should be involved at the highest (governance) levels dealing with important structural decisions and the lowest (patient care management) levels addressing day-to-day care in an exam room. Everything in the middle is management, and it should be handled by a professional team of experienced operational managers operating from a defined set of standards and objectives.

Chapter 15

Separate the Transactional Issues from the Transitional Process

The physician practice that is in transition is being impacted by any number of market and financial forces. It is characteristically understaffed, undercapitalized, and operating without a strategic vision or any kind of long-term plan. This comment is not meant to disparage any of the doctors that are working day to day to both operate a business and care for their patients. Understaffing and sparse capitalization are another way of saying that the practice is efficient from an operational perspective, and that the management is acutely aware of the risks of long-term capital commitment in a marketplace that is dominated by a few major purchasers in a form that might be considered oligopsony.* The purchasers all branch their pricing off the main fee reference source—Medicare. Information about fee schedules is relatively easy to obtain. This puts the doctor at a disadvantage from a purely economic perspective.

* This is the definition of a market in which there are only a few major purchasers, as opposed to an oligopoly, where there are a few major sellers of a product.

Practice Transition Does Not Follow a Recipe

The typical practice has been in transition since the practice was initiated. This is the concept of everything changing every time there is a change in the market. Practices are used to change, but it is change that is internally driven and not generally change that responds to an external force. There is often resistance, but this can be overcome by developing an initial plan. The physicians, in the contracting process, often assume that if their contracts are appropriate and the transaction is well structured, everything else will fall into place. Hospitals also make this same mistake.

It Is Not "Business as Usual"

The business of a health care practice falls into four categories of critical resources: the providers, the staff, the revenue stream, and the infrastructure. As the physician contracts change, everything else about the practice changes as well. It is helpful to identify a couple of major areas of concern within each category and then to address each area in more detail once the major risk areas are under control.

Providers

For the first category, one has to assume that the transaction and the physician and the provider contracts are in place and acceptable. The day after the practice transaction is executed, there will be doctors to care for patients, and this will continue as it did before the transaction. However, related to the issue of caring for patients is the question of whether the transaction might cause some kind of artificial* need for recredentialing. Major provider issues that also need to be addressed and coordinated may be the need for new contracts for malpractice. Chances are that these have been identified as issues and the technical processes are underway, but these are also issues that may impact patients, especially in the case of credentialing. An appropriate transition plan would anticipate how this needs to be relayed to the managed care plans and their subscribers. An effective transition program will assure that the managed care plans or the third-party payers are part of the process and that any recredentialing gaps are minimized and absolutely transparent to the patients. This often takes more than planning. It often takes some level of negotiation.

---

* The term *artificial* is applied here since the same providers are caring for the same patients, but they may be under a different corporate structure. If they are, the managed care plans may have regulations that require recredentialing simply because of the change of ownership. This may be a change that could take months to bring the doctors back into an arena where they can once again meet their patients in an environment that is sanctioned by a payer group.

The Staff

Related closely to the physicians are support staff members at every level. The transition plan assumes generally that staff will follow in line with the doctors, but this is a time when staff and key personnel may consider leaving the practice and moving on to another work environment or retiring. The loyalty to the doctor has been replaced by an institution, and the continuity of staffing is not something that can be taken for granted. Transition is smooth only if there is a ready complement of staffing to keep the patients flowing after the transaction. Generally, the many hours of interaction with the physicians are not matched by the type of planning that is necessary to properly coordinate staff issues. This may result in unnecessary tension at the time of closing as staff consider their options and lobby the doctors to try to correct what they perceive to be problems with moving from one organization to another. Another common problem is that the physician negotiations often occur at a level that is high enough so that modifications, if necessary, can be made during the process of negotiation. For the staff, there is less room for negotiation and the process is being conducted generally by a component of the administrative team that has not been directly involved in the overall negotiation process.

The staff will have questions, most of which can be anticipated. The challenge is to have enough discussion with them during the process of negotiation to involve them without investing a great deal of time in a transaction that might not actually be consummated. Some of the staff issues are pretty straightforward, and some can only be handled through some kind of planning process. The basics are: "Will I still have a job?" and "Will I still get paid at my present level?" Beyond these two are the obvious questions about the nature of the benefits and who will report to whom.

Many staff members may have built a relationship of trust with key physicians, and there may be some implied ownership of practice positions. Most important, it is essential to make sure that the staff stay in place at least in the near term. This means that it is necessary to do an inventory and to have sufficient HR resources ready to incorporate the staff within the health care structure in a timely fashion. Some areas of special challenge may be found immediately, and these should be addressed when the transaction is contemplated.

Nepotism should be dealt with directly. No employee should be incorporated into the new practice framework if he or she has a relationship with another employee, especially if it is in a supervisory or direct subordinate situation. This is especially true if there is a doctor-staff person relationship of some kind. There is no workaround. This is a recipe for future management problems, and it is a situation that does not conform to most health care institutions. Siblings, spouses, significant others, whatever one might call the relationship, should be discovered and discussed and deconstructed. If the parties are all capable in their performance of their role in the practice, there will generally be other opportunities within the health care system into which they can be moved.

Problem employees that are under some kind of cloud should be discussed, and they should be counseled in the transition process. These are employees who have traditionally underperformed and that the practice is in the process of coaching, or who should have been in some kind of coaching or counseling process. Simply put, it would be better not to transition these employees at all. However, one must understand that they have certain rights, and their employee rights with the practice may have legal implications for the doctors. These employees need to be identified and closely supervised. Hopefully, in the new management structure, they can thrive. If not, they will have to be handled like any other employee that is inadequate in his or her position.

Overcompensated employees have to be counseled regarding the newly established pay scales and job responsibilities. These employees may need to have their compensation scales adjusted, or they may need to be told that they are "red-lined." That is, their scales will not advance over time with inflationary steps that apply periodically for the rest of the staff. This will be in force until their salary of compensation fits within the schedules and ranges that have been determined for their job category.

Earned and unpaid *days off and accrued vacation time* can present a challenge since the health care system generally cannot account for these and must fit the employees into the HR structure that exists for the rest of the system. There may be a need for some kind of accounting assistance to the practice to help recognize this liability and deal with it. This is especially problematic in a practice that has worked under some kind of earned "comp time" program where employees have been allowed to "bank" or store up time that can later be taken as paid time off.

The Revenue Stream

The revenue stream issue is probably defined best by the type of transaction. In any deal, someone has produced some assumptions regarding revenue and maintaining this flow of income. However, there may not be a clear understanding of the role that managed care and payer groups may play in a situation where the physicians and providers change corporate structure. There also may be lag times built into handoffs from one billing staff to another or in the implementation of new registration systems or processing methodologies. Even a few weeks of interrupted revenue is going to have some impact that is significant to the new practice sponsor. If the physician revenue stream is directly affected, such as a transaction in which the doctors keep the accounts receivable, but the health system begins to bill and collect on their behalf, there will be political implications as well as financial.

In most cases, the solution is to recognize the revenue cycle management team that is in place and keep them and their procedures operating while minute changes are made in the transition from the process that has been traditionally in place to the new form of management or the new billing protocols. If the issue is credentialing of the providers and their ability to continue billing under a new tax ID number, there may be a form of transaction in which the former practice actually leases the providers to the new practice until the credentialing is established. This is a complex legal structure, and it is offered only as an idea that might be discussed to resolve a problem in an already resolved transaction. The leasing approach takes not only a sophisticated legal team, but also physicians who are committed to resolving a potential cash flow issue and a health care organization that has the capacity to perform interim bookkeeping and accounting functions to support this type of an arrangement.

Physicians who are undergoing reorganization are also having their billing stream reorganized as well. One of the parties actually "owns" this income stream and will suffer if it is interrupted. Challenges may occur with staff turnover, changes in IT, changes in credentialing through managed care plans, claims transmittal delays, registration, etc. Simply put, this is a part of the process that has to be managed. It cannot be a handoff. One person who has the experience and background to address moving a revenue cycle from one business enterprise to another must know that this is his or her job and that both organizations, physician and health system, are dependent upon his or her success.

Infrastructure

On the entire issue of infrastructure, the challenge is one of detail and obsession with detail. All of the contracts and service agreements in one business environment will be reconstituted in another. Some will not be assignable and will have to be reissued. The major challenges will be leased equipment, computer software, practice management systems, and service agreements. The team that is doing the transition should be operating from a central listing, and the major items that are going to be problems should be the ones that are addressed initially, but the items that have the most impact on the practice should be the ones that command the most resources. There is no sense working on copy machine leases if the software licenses for the practice management system are not in order.

Areas of focus should be related to registration, phones, intellectual property (web pages and linkages), software licenses, and leased equipment. Service agreements and warranties are also key items that need to be on someone's task listing. If there are service agreements for payroll processing, bookkeeping, banking, etc., they need to be addressed to assure that there is no interruption.

Table 15.1 simply demonstrates a grid that could be used for planning and the assignment of tasks. It is not complete; it is intended to show that each item has a date and *one person* assigned to each key area.

Table 15.1 Practice Transition Requires Excruciating Detail

No.	*Transition Issue*	*Due Date?*	*Assigned to?*
1	Establish a transition team attended by key physicians and management staff to define transition objectives and issues and to clarify assignments and authority.		
2	Develop a listing of all HR matters, including a full employee listing and assigned tasks and wage scales—before and after the transition. Perform an audit of unused vacation and personal leave days.		
3	Develop a listing of all contracts related to the practice and summarize the terms of each. This should include any terms related to assignability.		
4	Inventory all equipment and related service agreements. If there are leases, define how they can be transitioned and outline the terms of any buy-out. If these are related in any way to supply purchase agreements, they must be detailed accordingly and matched to the supply purchase commitment that is outstanding.		
5	Audit certifications, credentialing, accreditation records, licenses, and any other related processes that are external to the practice and determine how they can be retained and transferred.		
6	Detail the revenue cycle from billing to deposit status and assign a staff person to monitor each stage during the reorganization process.		
7	Develop and implement a written.... (You get the idea!)		

Approaching transition in this fashion will assure that nothing, or at least nothing that is mission critical, will be missed. Additional challenges may arise since a practice generally does not have or operate under the same standards that are found in a health care enterprise. Also, this is the time when the undiscovered issues within the practice will arise. These might include promises made to partners or employees and implied contractual relationships with vendors and suppliers. This is also a time when a vendor or a supplier will see a chance to change pricing structures and "improve" its contracting position at an increased cost to the health care enterprise.

Summary Issues

- Transition planning can become overwhelming if it is not organized and prioritized. The functions should be divided into areas that focus on the four pillars of a practice—providers, staff, revenue, and infrastructure.
- Generally, the health systems focus on providers and let the other areas maintain a status quo until the transaction is imminent. This is a mistake. Each critical support arena has to have direct oversight and a plan to move from the traditional processes to those that are complementary to the sponsoring organization—the health system.
- Transactions are not intended to keep everything "as is." They are done to foster and support system change. This will impact everything that surrounds the physician in his or her practice environment, and the idea of change should be identified as a key driver so that the physician can understand and support it.

Chapter 16

Establish Fundamental Standards and Link These Standards to Definitive Policies

In a recent *New York Times* article, it was noted that more and more physicians are moving to some kind of employment model.[*] A variety of reasons are offered, but they are pretty much summarized by the fact that employment looks much less risky than being in private practice these days. Yet, some physician practices are very well managed, and some financial indicators in private practice exceed those that could be achieved by a health care system. The time of transition is when these metrics can be muddled and lost. The battle cry in health care (one of them, anyway) is benchmarking. Best to get the benchmarks agreed upon up front and linked to policy statements that are clear and straightforward.

If physicians are fleeing private practice because they fear the future, should hospitals feel any less fear? Will consolidation and integration actually make up for some of the risk that physicians are feeling as they move from entrepreneurial situations to employment? Doubtful.

[*] Elizabeth Rosenthal, Apprehensive, Many Doctors Shift to Jobs with Salaries, *New York Times*, February 13, 2014.

Was the Practice Well Managed Beforehand?

Often the practice that is obtained through an acquisition is not a practice that is managed using clear business standards. This is not an officious way of saying that the practice was not well managed, but merely to imply that the doctors probably managed it "in the minute" and "on the fly." By some standards, it might have been "oddly managed" from the perspective of professional health care managers, but that may not mean that it was managed in an ineffective fashion. It might have been understaffed or undercapitalized. It might also have been structured to operate in a continuous peak loading mode. It might be suffering from all three forms of what a hospital might consider to be bad management, but it might also be optimized for revenue development and minimized for costs, which will produce the most net for the practice owner, the doctor.

Quality vs. Quantity and the Bottom Line

There is a natural division between administration and clinical duties—on paper. In reality, the idea of efficiency in management may broach on medical care because the manager is handling resources that might be used for the provision of that care. From the physician perspective, the idea of the practice environment is related closely to his or her clinical capabilities and if there is a deficiency, perceived or real, that needs to be addressed and fixed. This is also related to the timeless argument about short-term profit vs. long-term investment. From a purely business perspective, this is why most practices are undercapitalized. The capital allocation that a hospital would quickly make in an improved electronic medical record (EMR) is a difficult decision for a typical physician practice. The government has wisely made some provisions* for the offset of this cost, but not nearly enough for a 60-year-old doctor to be able to realize any kind of return.

The friction between the doctor who wants to have immediate access to whatever resource seems necessary at the moment and the hospital that needs to plan for a variety of resource needs is similar to the captain of a ship and the admiralty in the Navy. Onboard the ship at sea and in a battle situation, the captain is the key force in decision making. The doctor is at the bedside and in the exam room. However, there are limits to what can be provided from the government—for the defense budget and for the health care budget. General and macro resource constraints often define that for both the ship at sea and the community hospital. The differ-

* The offsets that immediately come to mind are the provisions for meaningful use and the safe harbor definition that the government offered to allow hospitals to invest in medical records systems for members of their medical staff without being exposed to regulatory sanctions.

ence is that the Navy has a tradition of some 200 years, and the hospital-physician integration process is still in a state of flux.

Managers Must Have Defined Roles and Responsibilities

If managers could manage intuitively, they would not need annual evaluations and job descriptions. If the management team is to be effective and stay on track, it needs to have its activities aligned with the goals of the organization, and if it is to be effective dealing with the doctors and the providers in the practice, it must have full knowledge of how the doctors are motivated in order to form a partnership in the practice that will produce results. This is not so difficult in a private practice where there is the ability for a doctor to walk down the hallway and admonish a manager directly. However, in a health care system where there is a scalar type of alignment that mirrors the military with captains and lieutenants responding to majors and colonels, this is more of a challenge.

The physician must be in some way incorporated within the manager's command structure, or if this is impractical, the doctor has to have a meaningful impact of some kind on the evaluation of the manager, and this has to be a known factor in the continuation of the manager's position and compensation structure. Simply put, the manager does not work *for* the doctors, but the manager must know that part of his or her job function is to closely align with the doctors and work *with* them to assure that they meet their own personal goals and objectives.

If a manager is charged with the functions associated with the physician enterprise, somewhere in his or her job description there should be a set of standards that foster a close working relationship with the doctors. The following principles are offered to the reader for consideration and as an example of the kind of language that should be part of every physician-oriented manager's job description.

Work directly with staff to develop an environment that, first, addresses patient safety and, second, assures physician efficiency and morale.

Assist with the determination of salary and bonuses of the providers (physicians) based on the established income distribution policy and on the doctors' contract terms.

Monitor individual physician production, collections, and expenses for potential changes that might impact overall practice performance and individual compensation levels.

Assists physicians and providers in achieving their optimal income potential under the guidelines defined for the practice and the contract provisions that define bonus awards and provider salary determinants.

Meet with physicians and providers on a regularly scheduled basis to elicit comments and suggestions on the way in which practice operations impact medical care standards and to assure that the doctors are aware of progress resolving issues that might have an impact on their practice environment.

Counsel physicians and providers regarding options available under benefits programs and institution-sponsored pension plans.

Review malpractice requirements, recommend changes when considered necessary, and meet with carriers and providers on all aspects of risk management related to the practice environment.

Monitor and implement programs to assure that the supplies and equipment necessary for the physician to operate effectively are in place and ready for any application that might be necessary.

Inserting these components in a management job description might be considered coddling an already privileged employee. However, the physician is an extremely valuable asset and represents the most costly input in the patient care process. The doctor has to have his or her role and status recognized and respected. If not, the cost of turnover and the erosion of any patient loyalty developed at great cost within the practice will prove to be the manager's eventual undoing.

There is a secret to managing clinical and physician-focused environments, and it is simply working daily on communication that clearly follows the model that supports the physician need for autonomy and effectiveness in direct patient management while eliciting input on the broader management issues that are operational and strategic. Generally, a balance between the immediate and the near term can be struck, which will allow a mutual level of respect for each party. The key is to recognize and celebrate the interdependence that exists between the physician and the practice support mechanisms that the health care system sponsors.

Is There a Clear Set of Achievable Metrics for the Practice?

Everyone should be operating from some kind of a dashboard reporting system. The overall top-end revenue is the driver for all other factors in the practice, and there are three simple questions that have to be answered by the team each and every day. How many patients did we serve? How many new patients did we serve? How many patients wanted service but were unable to be accommodated? If these numbers are not going in the right direction, the practice is in trouble.

Beyond the metrics, there are some pretty straightforward practice trend ratios that can be defined and shared with everyone so that they can gauge performance over time and without dealing with any kind of internal financial information. Financial measures are not the only thing to be measured. While this section focuses on numbers, there are also patient satisfaction and quality and effectiveness measures, all of which are key to the success of the organization. These will be addressed in a later section. They are critical, but they are more challenging to measure, and in some cases, the benchmarks are still emerging or are dependent upon the type of practice or organization that is deploying the doctors. However, the financial aspects relating to productivity transcend all health care delivery schemes.

Start with these overall indicators:

Number of new patients
Number of patients served
Staff hours per patient visit (nonphysician)
Overtime hours
Overall supply cost per patient encounter
Average waiting time per visit
Charts, records, claims returned for reprocessing

Frankly, in a health care situation, there is little else that is under the direct control of the practice. Rent and administrative overhead costs are determined at the corporate level, and overall practice top line (revenue) and bottom line (revenue minus expenses) are generally beyond the control of the practice unit, the staff at the practice level, and the physicians assigned to the site. However, direct patient care staff can all contribute to the metrics listed above, and they should all know that these are important measures.

Metrics that *should not* be posted and encouraged are those that are procedure related. There should not be a team effort (or even a team awareness) of the referrals for labs, pharmacy, imaging, or admissions or other revenue-related functions within the health care system. Reporting on these measures could border on compliance issues—both up and down. If the ratios are measured and moving up, then there is an implication that referrals and extra revenues are among the objectives of the practice, and if they are going down, it is an indication that there may be a focus on the overall restriction of services to this particular patient population. Volume indicators that are not directly related to patient satisfaction and efficiency measures should only be approached within the context of a recognized quality initiative, and then only if the program has been reviewed by compliance officers.

This does not mean that financials should not be reviewed by top management and overseen by accounting and financial staff. The following ratios have to be constantly in mind when there is a professional billing process and a revenue stream involved. Most managers will be familiar with these measures, but many hospital-based administrative staff will not be used to measuring them as frequently as necessary in a physician environment. Each should be charted monthly, and the trends should be identified by payer category so that there can be an immediate reaction if there is a significant fall off in any key category.

Accounts receivable ratio
Days in accounts receivable
Average monthly charges
Personnel expense ratios
Overhead ratio (nonprovider expenses)
Average charge per unit of service
Revenue generated by provider per month
WRVUs per provider per month[*]

Simply put, there should be a dashboard that forces comparative changes to be immediately recognized so that action or intervention can occur.

Are the Metrics Aligned with Management and Provider Compensation Models?

This is a simple question, but it is a complex process with many problems associated with the answers. The alignment of the compensation of the provider has to be coordinated with the goals of the organization. There are many forces beyond these metrics that are building in the provider community. These include the measures related to population management and risk assessment models and value measures. Any program that is simply based upon a measurement that is revenue oriented or focused only on cost controls is sure to become outmoded in the near future. Not only must one relate performance to financial indicators, but also there must be other measures that are balanced against pure financial models that link the practice and the doctors and managers to population management goals[†] and consumer satisfaction.

The challenge is to constantly assess the local payers and the consumer community to see how the metrics fit on an overall blend of compensation programming. In the old school practice, more patients and more services may have meant more money for the provider. Under new game plans, there will be bonus dollars available for

[*] WRVUs are work relative value units, which are emerging as a standard measure of physician and provider and practice productivity. They are defined for every conceivable Current Procedural Terminology (CPT) code that is allowed for a billable event by the Centers for Medicare and Medicaid Services (CMS). http://www.cms.gov/Regulations-and-Guidance/HIPAA-Administrative-Simplification/TransactionCodeSetsStands/CodeSets.html.

[†] Population management has emerged as a cliché, but it is rapidly becoming a discipline unto itself. The definition implies that the health care team can have its effectiveness measured by the health status of the population. Of course, the challenge is in defining the population and in measuring health status. Presently, this can be accomplished only by those organizations that have defined and distinct groups over which they have control (or manage risk). A health maintenance organization (HMO) is an example, as is an accountable care organization (ACO) or an employer that is self-funded for the care of its employees.

things like gain sharing* and value-based metrics. These opportunities are different right now from region to region and carrier to carrier, but they are going to become more well defined and universal as the Patient Protection and Affordable Care Act (PPACA) matures and more people join elective (and selective) provider groups.

Patient Service Process Measures and Patient and Consumer Satisfaction

It is not all about productivity; sometimes it is about performance. The eventual contract parameters will be about population management—actual effectiveness. The question is how to get from here to there. The answer is together and over time. Below are the transition stages.

Initially and in the first contract stage: Contract for individual availability and access and productivity. This means WRVUs, sessions, and call shifts. These are all easily quantifiable, and they all have references in the literature, and most importantly, they can all be easily benchmarked in contracts. At this stage, if it is possible, patient satisfaction scores can be added if they are already being collected and benchmarked. If not, they don't belong in an initial contract exhibit.

Second stage: Contract for personal effectiveness. This means that there can be additional steps to include things like citizenship, compliance with systems and protocols, timely and accurate processing of coding and billing, communication standards, etc. Some of these features in the relationship will become more subjective, but they can still be measured. The challenge at this stage is to design a contract form that is collaborative and which the providers accept as meaningful and achievable. This takes some level of communication and trust that a doctor coming into a joint venture with an organization, no matter what the form, may not accept in the first phase of the relationship.

Eventually: Contract on global and group performance. This means that the individual contract will now have features that will include some level of interdependence and collaboration. Again, this is not a problem to measure, but it is a leap of faith for an individual to link his or her pay to the performance of a group of colleagues that is dealing with a population of patients.

---

* *Gain sharing* is a term that is used to describe programs where cost savings are shared between the hospital and medical providers. CMS has published specific guidelines to assure that quality and access are basic to any program that rewards providers for efficiency or cost savings. CMS has to approve any type of gain sharing program that applies or involves the patient bases its covers. Hint: This means that almost every program needs to be reviewed. http://innovation.cms.gov/initiatives/Medicare-Hospital-Gainsharing/.

Starting out, this may mean using accreditation scores or patient health care indicators of some kind that are practice measured and not simply linked to an individual provider's behavior. On an interim basis, the standards can be blended over time to give the doctors some sense that they (and the group) will have time to learn how to impact the scores. This is not gaming; this is simply the way to move a group of individuals carefully and gently toward a common set of goals.

Metrics Can (Should) Change over Time

In the early stages of a relationship, where physicians are interrelating with a new organization or where they have transferred their full-time efforts from a private practice environment to one linked with the hospital, the measures for their involvement must be similar to what they are generally used to seeing. They come from a fee-for-service environment, and they are used to seeing cash reports and accounts receivable (AR) and patient process measures. The gentlest form of measure is a WRVU count, as long as they can understand what their historic production levels were in that same measure. Of course, hours dedicated to administrative time and call shifts and session assignments can also be a very straightforward and traditional measure.

Near term, the measures will be direct and under their immediate control and individualized. They may include scores for compliance with stated policies or adherence scores against medical treatment templates. They might include some measures of patient or peer satisfaction. They might include something like a citizenship factor.* In any case, they are beyond the simple productivity measures that prevail in most contracts, and this is necessary to move the physicians and providers from the fee-for-service mentality to the eventual linkage of payment for performance.

The stages that might be considered follow:

Stage 1: Payment for WRVUs removes any consideration of payer status. This takes the physician from focusing on dollars to focusing on work, and it makes the contract what is called payer neutral. That is, the Medicaid patient is the equivalent of the commercial patient.

Stage 2: Payment for factors that impact the practice environment and foster either efficiency or patient and colleague linkages. This dimension adds efficiency, consistency, satisfaction, citizenship, etc., to production. This moves

* Citizenship is a polite way of defining provider behavior, which will be detailed further in the Appendix. Suffice to say, at this point, the concept of two physicians working at the same pace and doing the same thing should be rewarded differently if one has more of an impact on staff costs and resources than the other. Citizenship measures those costs that are directly related to physician behavior as opposed to any form of clinical performance.

the provider beyond simple production and links its behavior and commitment to the enterprise to its compensation.

Stage 3: Payment for factors that reflect group performance. This is where things become challenging because metrics usually have to be defined and described to physicians in a way that will assure them that they actually have some kind of controls in place to impact change. The group can "do better" in any number of ways—financially and functionally. One way to start is to focus on group performance that is related to patient satisfaction or patient flow or access.

Stage 4: Payment for the improvement of the health status of the population. This is where you want to be, but it is not where a group can go immediately. The issue of productivity cannot be lost on this journey, nor can citizenship or group goals. This is a feature that should be added when all of the other indicators are pointing in the correct direction. Metrics abound. One might first start with those measures that are reflected in the literature and which have some implication for accreditation. These include HEDIS* measures as updated annually by the National Council on Quality Assurance (NCQA).

What about Financial Measures?

The problem with financial measures is that they are generally outside the physicians' immediate realm of control. Some are outside the control of the health system. If costs and revenues are going to be applied as group benchmarks, they need to be cleansed for the changes that are environmental. Heating and air conditioning costs are an example. If the cost of natural gas increases, the employed group of providers should not be at risk. If they are, the result will be doctors wearing sweaters and patients freezing. The same goes for reimbursement matters. The doctors probably sold their practice, or joined a health system, to avoid direct exposure to reimbursement risk. Nursing personnel are not directly exposed, and neither is the administrative team, but somehow doctors' contracts are sometimes constructed with reference to revenue and expense performance.

If the idea is to expose the providers to some kind of financial performance of the enterprise, this effort should be restricted to process measures that do not have to go through a bookkeeping mechanism of any kind. Ideas might include the general number of patients served by the group, the cost of overtime for the group, the staff hours per patient encounter, etc. On an individual basis, there is always the ability to benchmark against the group and to look at supply cost per patient or dedicated support personnel costs. If the practice is one that uses special

* Health Effectiveness Data and Information Set (HEDIS) as published annually by the National Committee for Quality Assurance. http://www.ncqa.org/HEDISQualityMeasurement/HEDISMeasures/HEDIS2014.aspx.

patient support for marketing or patient-informed consent, then these costs might be captured and applied to the doctors that have patients that directly benefit from the expenditures.

Summary Issues

- This is where good management must be supported by good contract development and a clear set of metrics that are understandable, quantifiable, and achievable. If any of these components are not present, the transaction will eventually need to be reformatted in some fashion.
- The goals are always general, and they are also pretty well agreed upon—quality, patient satisfaction, integration, and efficiency. These are not sufficient in the actual process of transition since they really are too general. There have to be specific objectives detailed under each goal so that all of the participants know the details of the journey that is being agreed upon.
- If the provider contracts are not in sync with the objectives, the process will fail.

Chapter 17

Align the Compensation with the Programming

When someone says that he or she is in a profession for the love of it and not for the money, this generally means that the money is probably either so low that it does not matter or so high that it is not any concern. However, if a change is proposed, the person who is the subject of the change (or the victim, depending upon the perspective) will immediately become very much engaged. A well-designed income determination process is essential. This must be something that has four factors as a basis for its development: (1) The salary and bonus must be competitive with the marketplace for the services and time commitment of the practitioner. (2) The compensation and the compensation model must have parity internally to other contracted providers. (3) The compensation must be linked to provider performance and exposed to factors in the marketplace. (4) The compensation must be related in some way to the objectives of the health system.

Dividing income between physicians in a group practice is always a challenge, and sometimes a contentious challenge. If a practice is a solo provider in a wholly owned business structure, the dollars go in the top end and the expenses are paid with everything that is left being used to pay the owner/provider/producer. It seems simple, but the simplicity masks the fact that the top-end revenue is dictated by the reimbursement environment, and the costs of employees and office expenses are defined by the marketplace. The owner (producer) can only work harder and produce more events under the traditional fee-for-service (FFS) system. Doctors who are in a group environment compete against the marketplace and the reimbursement pressures and often against their business partners. Legions have been written about the different ways that the practitioners can choose to take declining an amount of money—residual income—and divide it fairly among a number of hardworking doctors. Productivity is often combined with the equity or ownership composition and applied costs in some kind of a stew that has been designed by lawyers and accountants to get through the business process of rewarding owners for investment and producers for effort.

The factor that is not often realized in private practice is that there are significant risk factors, coupled with the issue that the owners have some amount of their own capital invested in the practice. If they had a true financial report on the practice, like most businesses do, they would realize that this capital has a value that could be realized in any number of investment channels. They would also realize that handicapping risk for any physician practice is a pretty difficult task in today's environment. However, this last fact is the very reason that many physicians are now moving from the private practice of medicine to one that is housed in a hospital system or which is a part of a corporate structure that can assume some of the risk.

The Hospital/Health System as Paymaster

The hospital or health system can take on some, but not all, of the risk of the income equation. However, there has to be some realization that if the sponsoring institution takes all the risk and the environment changes dramatically, the whole enterprise may be threatened. It is better to design some kind of a structure for physician compensation that allows the parties to move together through the various steps from fee for service to payment for quality and effectiveness. However, physicians and providers contract with hospitals, and a contract is a static relationship with regulatory oversight and, once written and executed, very little flexibility. Contracts that define determination methods that can respond to rapid change must take into account the local environment as well as the needs of the physician for contractual stability and the need to have a stable income. After all, why did the doctor come to work for the hospital in the first place? One of the reasons was to escape from the risks presented by rapid reimbursement change and the increasing costs and complexity of private practice.

There is no one best way to design a single type of structure that might address all of the needs of the hospital and the doctor, but this chapter will present a starting point for the development and design of a physician compensation system that may be able to be modified to suit most forms of contracting. Most of the suggestions are applicable to any type of medical practitioner, but some design concepts might need to be changed for specialties that are by their nature special cases. One size does not necessarily fit all, but some core ideas can be commonly applied. The footnotes will have specific ideas that might help in some specific areas and specialties. Income determination and the structure of physician compensation start with the idea that the physicians must understand and agree on the incentives that are built in to their compensation system. These incentives should reflect the mission or philosophy of the health care enterprise. Based upon a private practice orientation, very few practices simply divide income equally or pay a straight salary.* Most private practices that are large enough for a group practice designation divide income based upon partial productivity added to some kind of base salary. Some practices pay strictly on productivity.†

There will probably be inequities in any compensation system, but any system must be implemented with the understanding that the goal is to allow each provider to be rewarded on a basis that is equivalent to that used to reward all of the providers in the group without basing any part of the compensation on performance that is not within the power of the group (or the physician) to impact. Compensation systems must be tailored to fit the nature of the specialty and the practice. There should be a written schematic of some kind and the formulae and inputs should be transparent. Essentially, physicians or providers should be able to figure out how to advance themselves and their position and income, whether it is by individual effort or by the support of group goals.

These are some key elements that can be incorporated into a compensation system. These are not always desirable to include, but the list is offered to be complete.

Base salary (based on factors such as training and certifications)
Productivity (based on relative value units (RVUs), charges, or collections)
Recognition of marketing efforts (new referrals and patients)
Managerial/executive functions
Teaching assignments
Oversight of mid-level providers (physician assistants and nurse practitioners)
Call coverage
Patient satisfaction
Peer review assessments of physician clinical care
Tenure/seniority
Adherence to protocols
Quality measures
Citizenship issues

---

* Practices that pay on the basis of equal distribution of income are generally hospital-based group practices like anesthesia groups and radiology groups. This is generally to assure that there will not be an artificial competitive incentive for one doctor to select cases or shifts that have higher remuneration than his or her colleagues. Basically, the scheduling and the service levels of the group assure continued contract support, and internal competition might result in a variety of staffing and master contract performance issues.

† The cliché that goes with this method is the proverbial "Eat what you kill." This methodology supports pure competition at all levels of service, which certainly has some merit but which makes contracting for quality and effectiveness very difficult.

Contracts also contain many additional benefits that should never be confused with the process of defining income or offsetting any bonus or feature of compensation. These include coverage of malpractice, paid time off, professional dues and continuing medical education (CME), insurance coverage, pension, etc.

Some Basic Regulatory (and Commonsense) Constraints

The primary legal considerations in all physician compensation plans established by hospitals and any corporation that is a nonprofit enterprise or which deals with Medicare and insured patients include a variety of areas that need to be addressed. Simply stated, the income paid must be within a range of fair market value (FMV) in order to maintain the hospital's tax-exempt status by making certain that the amount of compensation and the method of payment do not jeopardize any regulations related to the tax-exempt status of the organization. Further, there can be no incentives for limiting care to Medicare recipients, nor can compensation be linked in any way to induce referrals.

This book, and this section, is not intended to be a legal reference for the reader since every contract and relationship should be reviewed by counsel familiar with the working regulatory structure in health care and the structure of legal constraints that exist on a state-by-state basis. Some generalities can be offered, however. One best practice is to always reference compensation to some external source. This may be published data and surveys, or it could be by obtaining a report from a consulting group that has its own regional and national databases. The key idea is to be able to justify the compensation package by referencing an external, objective, and unbiased resource if it is ever challenged. Incentive compensation is especially important to justify and monitor to make sure that there is not a contract form that allows or fosters some kind of egregious salary result for a provider (windfall), and to make sure that the compensation formulae support the overall health care mission and goals (if this is a charitable institution). Inducements of any kind that relate a physician compensation package to group performance that might include ancillary revenues or bonuses for referrals within the health care system can be suspect and should be avoided. Simply put, anything that channels referrals or allows a volume indicator to be used for anything except a physician's direct work effort should be scrutinized, as it is probably prohibited in some way.

Another challenge will be the opposite of inducements for volume and referrals. It will be the avoidance of incentivizing a physician to restrict or limit care to patients, especially Medicare- and Medicaid-covered individuals. This is especially tricky since the crux of efficiency is applying just enough (but not too much) care when it comes to diagnosis and treatment. Of course, physicians who are good at determining the right level of care should be rewarded for their expertise, but this has to be done in a measured and purposeful way and described in contracts that recognize the balance between effective and efficient medical care and the rationing of care or the restriction of services to vulnerable groups.

A good rule is to have a set of rules. That is, there should be a compensation committee of some sort that operates under board guidelines and which has access to the necessary tools (and experts) who can guide general policy. Institutions get in trouble when contracts and deals are "one off" or individualized. If there is a guide set of some kind or an oversight committee that can provide some level of internal consistency, the process will be relatively risk-free.

The more objective the process is, the better it will serve all of the constituencies in the mix. The more subjective it is, the more risk of conflict and oversight. Again, an attorney with transaction experience in health care with specific knowledge of the individual state in which the contract is being executed and maintained should be the final arbitrator on form.

One Model, Many Factors

Figure 17.1 is a unified approach to physician compensation based on several factors relating directly to an income determination model. The reader should not be put off by its complexity—it is actually pretty simple, and it is intended for a small group of five doctors operating in a captive PC mode or as a unit within a health care system that can be charged with some overall group responsibility and individual decision making. The model is meant to foster physician-informed participation in a number of factors that are key to the operation of the practice unit as well as directly involve them in the overall performance of the sponsoring institution (at least at their level of operations).

The basic issue for the organization is the question of top-end revenue and its balance against expenses. This practice unit has the top-end revenue in the upper-left-hand corner. This number could also be reflected as a productivity indicator, like work relative value units (WRVUs). However, in some fashion, the doctors should be kept informed of what the overall revenue production of their unit activity represents (see Figure 17.2). This may not flow into their own personal paycheck, but it helps them to be informed when decisions need to be made concerning the addition of new providers or changes in the reimbursement structure overall. One will note several other factors reported in the upper-left-hand part of the income schematic.

The chart contains information and adjustments that are related to reported overhead (60%) and other revenues ($120,000), as well as a factor for billing and the costs of benefits and CME/travel. These are all meant to inform the doctors about the revenues that might be additive to any fee-related billing and to expose them to a running report on expenses. In keeping with the theme of having doctors make determinations on many of the areas under their direct control, there are only a couple of areas in this portion of the chart that might be immediately impacted by the physicians—one is general production and the other is the category labeled

Revenue, Annualized	**3,750,000**	
Overhead Factor	60.00%	
Number of Physician FTEs	5.00	
Distribution for Physicians	1,500,000	Unadjusted
Ancillary/Other Residual	120,000	
Billing Expense	8.02%	
Net, available for Distribution	1,490,000	Pending elective adj.
Related Costs (misc.)	(60,000)	
Benefits/Pension	(75,000)	15,000 per doctor
CME, Travel	(15,000)	3,000 per doctor
Net, available for distribution	1,340,000	
Fixed Stipends	(1,000,000)	From contracts, base pay
Administrative	(40,000)	Determined by contract
Residual (to be distributed)	300,000	

Related Costs—Group Level	**($60,000)**
Holiday party	2,000
Cell phones for doctors (elective upgrades)	2,000
Golf and gymnasium memberships	12,000
Sponsored educational seminar (retirement)	1,000
Donation to the Medical Staff Development Campaign	5,000
Donation to the House Officers' Recreation Fund	1,000
Cakes and decorations for staff birthday parties	0
Purchase of artwork for individual offices	12,000
Furniture for physician lounge upgrade	12,500
Physician lab coat purchase and laundry	10,500
Petty cash	1,000
Other	1,000

							170	*Total Points*			
			100		*50*		*20*	*Points*			
		58.8%		29.4%		11.8%					
	1,000,000	*176,471*		*88,235*		*35,294*		*40,000*		*1,340,000*	
	Fixed/Mkt. Adj.	Production?		Call/Other?		Citizenship?		Administration		Salary	
Doctor 1	270,000	2,100	45,752	3	2,322	1	11,765	1.00	26,667	$356,505	27%
Doctor 2	250,000	3,000	65,359	45	34,830	1	11,765	0.00	0	$361,954	27%
Doctor 3	230,000	1,800	39,216	34	26,316	0	0	0.50	13,333	$308,865	23%
Doctor 4	150,000	1,200	26,144	32	24,768	1	11,765	0.00	0	$212,676	16%
Doctor 5	100,000	0	0	0	0	0	0	0.00	0	$100,000	7%
Totals	*1,000,000*	*8,100*	*176,471*	*114*	*88,235*	*3*	*35,294*	*1.50*	*40,000*	*$1,340,000*	
	74.6%		*13.2%*		*6.6%*		*2.6%*		*3.0%*	*100.0%*	

Figure 17.1 Physician income must address both external and internal realities. (To download this worksheet, visit www.medicalstaffintegration.com)

Revenue, Annualized	3,750,000	
Overhead Factor	60.00%	
Number of Physician FTEs	5.00	
Distribution for Physicians	1,500,000	*Unadjusted*
Ancillary/Other Residual	120,000	
Billing Expense	8.02%	
Net, available for distribution	1,490,000	*Pending elective adjusted*
Related Costs (misc.)	(60,000)	
Benefits/Pension	(75,000)	*15,000 per doctor*
CME, Travel	(15,000)	*3,000 per doctor*
Net, available for distribution	1,340,000	
Fixed Stipends	(1,000,000)	*From contracts, base pay*
Administrative	(40,000)	*determined by contract*
Residual (to be distributed)	300,000	

Figure 17.2 Develop revenue and adjustments to revenue.

"related costs/misc." This is a catchall category to allow physicians to determine how much they might want to allocate from their budget to "optional" (but important) discretionary spending, which will be described more fully on the following pages.

The top-end revenue can be actual reported revenue or it can be an adjustment from a WRVU computation.* In any case, this is the area where the doctors get to see what they are producing as a group. Ancillary revenue is something that can come from anywhere—quality bonus incentives, payments for meaningful use,† research revenues, or any kind of revenue that is not specifically tied to any one doctor or related specifically to fee-for-service reimbursement of care.

Whatever the source of the numbers, it is important to be able to link it to physician group productivity and physician group performance overall. The use of a conversion factor or some kind of revenue component will also allow the program to be linked to external market forces, with the caveat that once this is done, these forces can pressure contract terms in either a downward or an upward fashion.

* This would be done by defining a conversion factor that could be used for a reference against the market or the numbers in the doctors' original contracts. The number of WRVUs times the conversion factor would be the resulting revenue. This approach insulates the doctors from issues concerning patient payer mix and hospital performance as a collection agent.

† *Meaningful use* is a term that describes a bonus system physicians receive for the successful implementation of electronic medical records. Any form of quality indicator or group gain sharing bonus could be added as a part of the top-end revenue in order to allow an individual physician to be recognized for group performance as well as for individual production efforts.

Related Costs—Group Level	*($60,000)*
Holiday party	2,000
Cell phones for doctors (elective upgrades)	2,000
Golf and gymnasium memberships	12,000
Sponsored educational seminar (retirement)	1,000
Donation to the Medical Staff Development Campaign	5,000
Donation to the House Officers' Recreation Fund	1,000
Cakes and decorations for staff birthday parties	0
Purchase of artwork for individual offices	12,000
Furniture for physician lounge upgrade	12,500
Physician lab coat purchase and laundry	10,500
Petty cash	1,000
Other	1,000

Figure 17.3 Allow adjustments for some elective categories.

This next category (which ends up being $60,000 in this example) contains many items that are not guaranteed by contract but which might be considered highly desirable by the doctors. This is an offset to the availability of income available for distribution. Putting these expenses in this format allows them to be incurred by the practice unit on a pretax basis. The doctors get the benefit, but they also pay for it (Figure 17.3). The extra effort to structure an income determination program in this fashion emulates private practice and creates a sense of empowerment among the providers.

Actually, it is real empowerment and not just the sense of empowerment that is necessary to fuse physician commitment with an institutional set of goals. The rest of the spreadsheet follows in a format that fosters true transparency and which allows the doctors to understand how much they can impact their own income by achievement of predetermined performance standards. The open manner in which this is communicated to the doctors will assure that there is a complete level of understanding, and if there is internal parity, it will also assure some level of support by the majority of the participants.

In Figure 17.4, the doctors are all contracted for a certain base amount that adds up to a million dollars. The way it is presented assures that they understand that adding an additional provider will be something that has to be taken from the amount that is available for distribution, and that all costs have to be covered, including their benefits and base salaries, before there is any distribution related to individual performance or production. In this case, the allocation of the remaining dollars ($300,000) is distributed among categories that are related to production, call, citizenship, and administration. Many categories could be discussed, but these are ones that are easily discussed in any group of doctors since each understands

		58.8%		*29.4%*	
	1,000,000	*176,471*		*88,235*	
	Fixed/Mkt. Adj.	Production?		Call/Other?	
Doctor 1	270,000	2,100	45,752	3	2,322
Doctor 2	250,000	3,000	65,359	45	34,830
Doctor 3	230,000	1,800	39,216	34	26,316
Doctor 4	150,000	1,200	26,144	32	24,768
Doctor 5	100,000	0	0	0	0
Totals	*1,000,000*	*8,100*	*176,471*	*114*	*88,235*
	74.6%		*13.2%*		*6.6%*

Figure 17.4 Apply production factors and quality or any other contract features. This table shows two of the variables from Figure 17.1: production and call.

immediately where he or she might fall in any formula that is derived from this type of a model.

The computations are simple—gross revenue minus direct expenses will yield pool dollars available for distribution. When one takes the contracted base amounts of pay, there is a sum that is left that can be used for any type of incentive that has been defined.

One area that bears some additional discussion in the first column is the idea of doctors who work more or less time than the norm. Examples like job sharing and doctors being asked to work extra shifts come immediately to mind. A way to modify this column is to base it on a number of standard shifts and give a value for each. This might mean that if the doctor is being paid a base of, say, $200,000 per year and there is an expectation of having that doctor in the clinic for scheduled patient access time for something like 400 half-day shifts, then a trade-off for time in the clinic would be $500 per shift. This does not mean that the doctor can work on a self-scheduled basis; it only means that there is a predetermined adjustment that can be made for a necessary, predicted, and coordinated change up or down in a schedule. When this type of flexibility is anticipated and designed into the compensation scheme, the potential for future confusion is minimized.

Call Compensation and Confusion

The idea of call coverage has always been "baked in" to a physician's work schedule and patient and practice responsibilities. Radiology techs in a hospital got "call pay," and the radiologists worked out a call schedule for their time that assured the department was covered. Call was assumed as being part of a practice, and if doctors wanted to be on the medical staff of a hospital, they committed to being on call for not only their own patients, but also for their department or discipline. There are now doctors who cover the hospital (hospitalists), and contracts are being written with doctors that specify the amount of call and the type of call for which they will be responsible. The column that reflects call simply recognizes that this practice sets aside a certain proportion of available compensation (in this case, $88,235) and divides it among those doctors who take call for the group. These dollars are distributed on a percentage basis to whoever logs the call days for which they are designated. The example, right or wrong, has something like 6% or 7% of the overall compensation benefit reserved for this component of the income equation.

Because of the rise of hospital-hired doctors, the idea of call pay has now come into discussions relating to physician compensation and contracting. Surveys that traditionally reported on physician compensation simply assumed that the doctors reporting were being compensated for "all time and all effort," which would include call and any other function that was necessary to maintain a patient base and support a practice. This would also include medical staff meetings and administrative functions. In the last few years, hospitals have had to quantify what they want their staff doctors to do—manage departments, assist with accreditation, train support staff, and take calls. This has now made call coverage a unique and separate part of a contract discussion with the result that some coverage is now valued on a per shift basis.

The idea of shift coverage and call pay is also prevalent among some of the subspecialties that are required for key designations, like that of a trauma center. Examples are neurosurgery and orthopedics. Of course, once there is one specialty paid on a per shift basis, it is likely that other specialties will become award and demand payment. The hospital is caught between a rock (EMTALA*) and a proverbial hard place—the medical staff.

As a general strategy, it seems reasonable to support the compensation of physicians for call services in instances where it may: (1) contribute to the professional competence level and responsiveness of physicians providing call services to a facility and its emergency department patients, (2) improve efficiency of the emergency department, (3) assure the delivery of high-quality care to emergency department patients, including some who may be uninsured or underinsured, (4) prevent a loss of coverage or gap in service that limits a broad community benefit due to available medical personnel or medical staff members that no longer wish to take calls, and (5) assist and assure that a hospital can comply with accreditation and certification processes and regulatory responsibilities.

---

* EMTALA is the Emergency Medical Treatment and Active Labor Act, which governs how a Medicare participating hospital may refuse treatment to a patient (hint: they can't refuse a patient treatment) and when a patient might be transferred from one hospital to another institution.

Establishment of per diem rates of call according to the *Supplemental Compliance Guide for Hospitals*[*] outlines special challenges related to determining fair market value. Physicians in certain high-demand, high-burden call specialties (including neurosurgery, OB/GYN, and orthopedics) might be paid a stipend, especially in underserved markets, to assure full call coverage. The appendix contains a more complete discussion of a call policy that might assist governing bodies in defining and determining whether call subsidies might be appropriate.

Putting It All Together

In the bottom segment of Figure 17.1, the doctors have columns for administrative coverage and for a thing called citizenship. The administrative component is pretty straightforward since it follows an organizational chart and a job description. In the interests of transparency, this is a factor that is put right up front so that the doctors can be informed of the costs of having one of their own perform management functions on behalf of the medical enterprise. This is worthwhile since the administrative functions can become part of the overall evaluation process in which the doctors will be asked to participate. When they realize that there is a fund that is created from which administrative dollars are being subtracted, the idea of evaluating their colleagues for the administrative work they perform becomes much more meaningful.

The idea of citizenship might be a little more elusive, but once it is explained to physicians, it is generally an idea that they support. The concept is that the behavior of a specific doctor can actually cost the group in time and expense and in enterprise-wide prestige. Every doctor can give examples of how this might have impacted the process of patient care. Incomplete charts, late starts in the clinic, unresponsive call physicians, etc., are all examples of performance problems that cost the practice in some way. The appendix contains an example of a policy that might be used for implementing a policy on citizenship that ties into a bonus structure.

In summation, the model that has been suggested is one that is simpler than many but more complex than the standard income determination processes used with doctors contracting in most of the current scenarios. The physicians, once removed from the business of running their own practice, will see all top-end revenue through the lens of the contract, and unless they have some linkage to the realities of the marketplace, when the changes to a more capitated- (or quality- or efficiency-) driven process emerges, they will continue to follow the contract and not the future. The hospital will be stuck with a group of doctors acting exactly as they have been contracted to perform.

---

[*] *Federal Register*, Volume 70, Number 19, January 31, 2005, Notices, 4858, 4866.

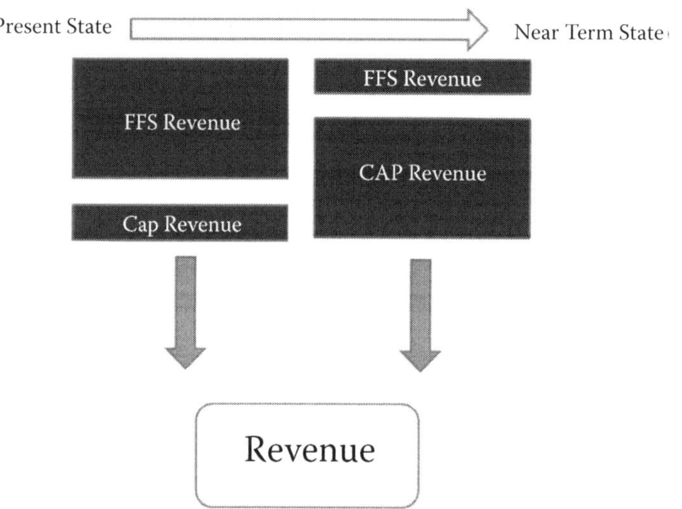

Figure 17.5 Fee-for-service revenue is being replaced by capitated forms of payment for medical services.

Figure 17.5 shows the change from FFS to capitation-oriented revenue. From the physician perspective, all revenue is homogeneous when it is filtered through a contract that is insensitive to the nature of the marketplace, which makes the source of the dollars irrelevant.

Summary Issues

- A good contract has an income determination process that is stable enough to attract physicians yet flexible enough to allow change as the marketplace changes from a fee-for-service environment to one that is more related to quality and effectiveness and capitation.
- The physicians must know how to "win." The inclusion of significant components of a contract payment structure that is related to features other than productivity is key to being able to alter the contract terms over time so that everyone can win.
- The goal is not to hamper the physician's creativity or involvement in revenue generation and cost control (at the practice level), but to give him or her a channel for involvement and the information on which he or she can make a good decision.

- The WRVU model is essentially a fee-for-service model that is payer neutral. Any institution that wholly bases the pay of doctors on productivity will be trapped with a group of doctors that can only win by doing more. This is going to become a trap for the administrative team that is only trying to keep the physicians pushing patients and procedures when the marketplace turns toward more sophisticated contract forms.

Chapter 18

Developing a Core Set of Strategic Issues

Very few health care providers follow any kind of commonsense pattern for the acquisition of practices or the incorporation of practices into the overall fabric of care through whatever form of integration is used. The physician-hospital organization (PHO) becomes defined by whichever practices sign up. The medical staff is the pool for recruiting practices to be integrated more formally (purchased), or worse, the practices are engaged when they knock on the door and wish to be acquired.

A more formal process might be described in Figure 18.1. Start with the end goal in mind and there may be a chance that it can be achieved. Respond to requests and the danger is that there will be no result that is workable.

Form does not always follow function in the purchase of a practice or the inclusion of a physician in a structured employment agreement. There are many competing factors, and they may seem to be overlapping in nature, but each has to be studied in detail and at a level of specificity that allows a clear decision by the appropriate stakeholder—physician as well as health system. Each has its own form of financial optics.

The transaction also must be structured on a business platform that is internally consistent with how the sponsoring health care enterprise conducts business. It has to have some kind of anchor to the overall sponsorship of the organization and its goals and objectives—as a business and as a part of the entire enterprise. The transaction has to be appealing to the physicians and meet their financial objectives in the short term and their security objectives in the longer term. The transaction has to clear regulatory hurdles and be compliant in all respects with standards that are becoming increasingly tight concerning the definitions of fair market value and

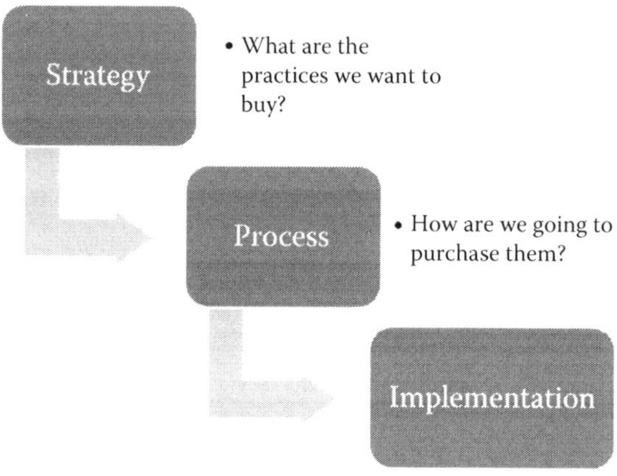

Figure 18.1 Without an overall strategy, the process will have no definition.

commercial reasonableness. Finally, the transaction has to be something that makes business sense to the institution that will be the host of the final practice or provider operation. So, there are four hurdles to meet: attractive to the seller, attractive to the buyer, compliant with regulators, and internally consistent.

Visions and Hallucinations

Planners and stakeholders involved in system design should develop some basic rationale that supports the overall idea of pursuing transactions and which describes the advantages generally to each entity. This is a philosophical base on which to continue the discussions both internally and externally. Essentially, why are we doing this? Why are the doctors seeking a partnership?

Economics of scale and efficiencies in the application of capital?
Coordination and improvement of patient access or patient care?
Enhanced ability to recruit doctors to the community?
Improved information, management, better cost control?
Improved market position for each participant?
Reduced risk?
Development of future businesses or product lines?
Preparation for the emerging managed care environment?

Many reasons would be considered appropriate, but there is one that is not a reason that makes sense: This would be some kind of a joint venture or transaction to rescue a failing practice; another would be the acquisition of one that is unable to be repositioned for the future.

Succession Planning

There are many elder statesmen (and stateswomen) from the medical staff who do not have a practice that can be transitioned to a younger practitioner and who cannot recruit any new talent. The model changed on their watch. They purchased into a practice when the reimbursement and physician recruitment environment was more favorable, and now they cannot use the same tools their predecessors used to recruit them. The general name given to this type of program that elevates it to the planning level is succession planning. Consultants cull through the medical staff and pick out the older practitioners and make the assumption that they will be the ones that can be enticed to transition their practices within some kind of structure that is more like an integrated model. Actually, this is a correct assumption, but generally for the wrong reasons. These practices are certainly good to approach, and the doctors may wish to sell, but they are also probably undercapitalized, and the expectations of the doctors-in-residence may not be in line with what the health system may need, or what it may want to pay for what it needs. There is a reason these practices have become unable to repopulate themselves with newer and younger doctors.

Generally, in the construction of an integrated system, the idea of secession planning is not one that will provide a base plan for success. It is one important component of a medical staff planning function, but it should not be the core component of the effort. The need is for new practices, right sized and properly placed to be able to engage the new consumer market demands.

Structure?

Determine the final *structure* that best complements the practices that are going to be recruited and the sponsoring health care system. Again, this is preplanning and not necessarily something that should be left to determine when the doctors are in the waiting room area with their financials. Will this be a sponsored PC, a management services organization (MSO) model of some kind, a foundation model clinic with teaching at its core, or some sort of joint venture? Each has different characteristics, and other chapters in this book should give you a way to look at each of the models and their relative strengths and weaknesses.

For whatever form is desired, the *legal structure and approvals* must be defined. Set up the overarching legal framework, and it might also be very helpful to draft some of the acquisition or integration documents. The attorneys may caution that this is premature, but this is a planned process and not a negotiation. If the documents are 90% ready, the discussions with doctors will go much more quickly and efficiently.

Financial Issues, Systems Level

Financial feasibility must be performed to assure that the arrangement meets standards of prudence and sound fiscal policy for all the organizations involved on a case-by-case basis. However, before a health system starts on this venture, it should have the financial wherewithal to do the following:

- Purchase or fund a sufficient number of transactions to make a market impact with the resulting practitioners
- Sustain the practices through a phase of ramp-up that includes recapitalization and reorganization
- Have sufficient funds on hand to cover initial operations while the reimbursement processes catch up to the transactions*
- Recognize what second- and third-year projections of cost and loss should be, as these years would be the periods in which staffing and programs are undergoing major changes, all of which might be categorized as investments, but each of which will definitely be a need for cash

When the overarching finances are not planned upon and available, the enterprise (PHO? MSO? or whatever) becomes a significant cost on the parent, and the result is to treat it like any other department. Managers are motivated to push revenue and hold costs, and this may be a natural process for a hospital, but it is one under which the integrated medical model will fail. If the global level planning has been done and the realization is that there will be short-term investment (cash shortfall) and long-term gain (in covered lives and capitated or contract revenue), the project may have a chance.

Specific and Special Opportunities

The initial discussions notwithstanding, there is nothing that will really be done in the development of a PHO or an accountable care organization (ACO) or an independent provider association (IPA) or a practice purchase unless there is an

* Often, after a transaction occurs in which there is a corporate change of some sort, the reimbursement process must begin again with the credentialing of practitioners and the qualification of the practice to serve a particular covered population. This can take 3 to 9 months depending upon the carrier(s), and this time period will have a very constrained revenue stream that is often misjudged by the acquiring entity.

engagement at both the philosophical and the financial level. Function can follow these two arenas of potential agreement. Broadly speaking, the philosophical and vision part of the programming will be either the recognition of common goals (or fears) or the development of a governance structure that allows everyone meaningful participation. However, the financial process is well defined and starts with mutual *due diligence*. Discussions should be very precise over operational issues vs. governance issues. In the initial stages, there should be some basic understanding of how decisions will be made.* This may involve other parties and constituencies, and these should be identified up front. An example is the presence of a union in a health care corporate environment. The idea that there will be an insulation of the practice from the pressures of unionization should be discussed in realistic terms.

Special standards that might not be present in the traditional practice should also be discussed. These include the idea of staff parity and wage and salary guidelines and overall compliance standards that might exist in a hospital but which a private practice might not consider in its traditional setting. If accreditation is to be a goal, this should be addressed and added as part of the planning discussions.

Decisions that might be otherwise collaborative would become subservient to the fact that the Joint Commission or AAAHC† criteria are going to be used for the development of standards within the practice. It is helpful, while the process is underway, to draw an organization chart and to develop job descriptions (even in abbreviated formats). If there are committees that are deemed to be necessary, their roles should be carefully defined.

Issues Listing—One Approach

Assuming that there is a policy and a plan for the integration of the independent practices, in whatever structure, there should be a process for linking them with the business enterprise. This is not about buying a practice; it is about choosing a partner in an awkward three-legged race to capture lives under new reimbursement

* The relationship between religious-sponsored groups and private practices offers special challenges. Most people relate this to the Catholic hospitals and the American Conference of Bishops and their admonitions against birth control and abortion. However, there are any number of religious-oriented practices and health systems. Many have ideas that are important to take into account when fashioning an arrangement of any kind. These include sponsorship by organizations that have the core beliefs of Adventists and Jews as well as Catholics. Also, one has to take into account that these beliefs extend to end-of-life care and research as well as women's services.

† The Joint Commission (http://www.jointcommission.org/) and the Accreditation Association for Ambulatory Health Care, Inc. (https://www.aaahc.org/) are both accreditation agencies frequently cited in the literature and in practice in certifying the quality of outpatient health service providers.

structures. The following list can help in the prequalification process. There must be some level of agreement on these issues before the process is undertaken.

1. What is the baseline production level anticipated for each practice site on a provider-specific basis?
2. Is there full agreement that all ancillaries should be centralized and contracted at the business enterprise (parent) level?
3. Is there a compensation methodology that assures internal parity and external competitive salaries and bonuses?
4. Is there a reasonable expectation of provider stability and consistency? This means restrictive covenants or noncompete portions of any proposed agreements as well as a replacement plan for upcoming retirees.
5. Is there an appropriate insurance coverage plan (malpractice) in place for both the parent business and each business unit and the individual providers?
6. Are the practice units in areas where community need studies have shown that there exists high potential for utilization?
7. Is there a process for the inclusion of mid-level providers in areas where they can contribute to the overall success of the venture?
8. Is there a strategy for the unification of registration and medical records that is workable and affordable? Have the providers committed to this idea?
9. If this is to be a transaction that impacts employees (practice sale or MSO), have the HR issues been addressed and is there a transition plan in place to assure that there will be a high capture of trained and "in place" staff?
10. If the transition involves employees, is there a process for transitioning their benefits, including their paid time off credits?
11. Has there been clear discussion about governance and management structures and who is in charge of what?
12. Is there some plan for the transfer of intellectual property and trademarks to benefit the business enterprise? Can the system ownership benefit in any way from existing websites, social media, and past provider advertising?
13. Are accounting and financial controls and any reporting system interrelationships defined? Are policies consistent between sites?
14. Is there a communication plan (both external and internal)?

If these questions cannot be answered positively, the parties should pause and reconsider whether they are ready for a transition that will be challenging at every stage. This process is like marriage counseling in a way, where a knowledgeable and experienced guide can outline some of the issues, but the two parties are lusting after the consummation of the process. The level of listening and reason can be drowned out by the desire to get the deal accomplished.

The new enterprise will be entering the marketplace with reduced revenues (initially) and new policies and procedures. There is a significant risk of losing key staff, and with them some significant talent and experience. There are many costs that will be new and unanticipated if there is not any thoughtful planning. All of these problems can be mitigated if the groups pause for a moment in the midst of all the contracting noise and simply outline the issues, assign them to staff, and address them on a prioritized basis.

Summary Issues

- Planning has to be part of the process. Sometimes the plan is simply to respond to competitive pressures.
- Hospitals are subject to reactionary planning and so are doctors. This mix makes for bad outcomes. There are some key ingredients to the development of an enterprise that will be core to any process—chaotic and precipitous or chaotic and well planned.
- Establish standards and stick to them. A good contract is not a good plan, and a key acquisition in which the transition is hurried and ineffective will have an impact that will take years to overcome.
- Set standards for any partnership and determine some core issues that must be met before moving forward.

Chapter 19

Is There a Clear Value Proposition?

This is pretty intuitive, unless it is something that everyone forgets. The common value propositions for all parties go something like this:

- The parties wish to reduce risk by collaboration in some form that will have a critical mass that can impact costs.
- The parties wish to improve market position by establishing a contracting platform that is meaningful to the market and responsive to emerging reimbursement trends.
- The parties wish to pool expertise and information in order to form more effective and efficient models of care.
- The parties wish to create a patient base that can be served effectively and will in turn be a loyal customer base on which planning and capital formation can be approached with confidence.

Quality and consumerism and Patient Protection and Affordable Care Act (PPACA) notwithstanding, this is about making an organization that the market cannot ignore—the construction of which is painful, but the result of which is a team of health care professionals that cannot be ignored by contracting agencies and managed care plans. The value proposition for the hospital is survival, and the value proposition for doctors is income stability and professional satisfaction.

What is the value proposition for the community and contracting bodies? Simply put, it is access to care and a channel for progressive care from one level of the health system to the next at a cost that is not excessive. This will necessitate a

OFFICE-BASED	COMMUNITY-BASED	HOSPITAL PROGRAMS	REGIONAL CENTERS	NATIONAL REFERRALS
PCP'S				
PEDIATRICS				
OBSTETRICS/GYN				
INTERNAL MED.				
	CARDIOLOGY			
	PULMONOLOGY			
	ALLERGY			
	GEN. SURGERY			
		GI		
		ORTHOPEDICS		
		ONCOLOGY		
		DERMATOLOGY		
		NEUROLOGY		
		UROLOGY		
		OTOLARYNGOLOGY		
		ENDOCRINLOGY		
			SUR. ONCOLOGY	
			COLON RECTAL	
			VASCULAR	
			PALLIATIVE CARE	
			NEUROSURGERY	
			NEONATOLOGY	
			MATERNAL FETAL	
			CARDIAC SURGERY	
			NEPHROLOGY	
			SPECIALTY PEDS	
			BEHAVIORAL	
				HEART TRANSPLANTS
				GENETICS

Figure 19.1 Ratios and stages are critical for value-based networks (narrow networks).

business model that is just big enough and not too expansive and a network that is "right sized" for the marketplace. The primary care piece is dependent upon geography and consumers, but the specialty pieces are dependent upon the primary care base. Figure 19.1 shows how this might be conceived. This chart ignores the obvious hospital-based specialties like radiology and pathology and some of the hard-to-define specialties like ophthalmology. It may not fit every case, but it should be discussed in every situation because the practices that are organized around a network of any kind will be arrayed in local neighborhoods and regional locales. When necessary, they will be hospital based. If a group is planning some form of a delivery system, it should know that those who plan networks start with this type of a schematic in mind.

This is not the standard medical staff structure—it is a group practice structure or a staff model health maintenance organization (HMO) structure. It is a structure that has enough access at every level to assure that patients will be able to see a doctor when necessary in a specific specialty, and that the doctors will have enough pathology to keep up their skills and justify their earnings.

Summary Issues

- Planning includes a variety of value propositions. Collaborative planning in health care includes community planning and planning to meet population health needs.
- Not every hospital or health system has every service available—nor should they. However, every network has to be structured to afford the patient access to every part of the health care system.
- Planners should start with the most complex and work backward. Most groups will agree that national centers are the only ones that can handle some types of cases
- The definition of what patients may need what type of care and where that care should be delivered is the most sophisticated level of planning, and it is only achieved by the most mature and confident of health systems.

Chapter 20

Build an Organization That Can Learn and Transform Itself

The initial idea of questioning the business case process behind this chapter was driven from experiences in many urban markets where physician practices were purchased and then "given back" or abandoned by the sponsoring institution. This happened with a many of the major PPMCs* a couple of decades or so ago.

Hospitals fail to achieve a clear understanding of the business cases associated with medical enterprises for a number of simple reasons. First, they do not have the same accounting and financial standards as a private practice, and second, they fail to plan for the costs that are incorporated within their own organization that are being avoided by the private practitioner. The result is generally a set of projections that are unreliable. Another issue is that the hospital or health system fails to look upon a practice or a group of practices (or management services organization (MSO) or physician-hospital organization (PHO) or accountable care organization (ACO)) as an ongoing investment. The PPMCs were able to go back to the equity

* PPMC is the acronym for physician practice management company, the most famous of which was PHYCOR, which consolidated physician practices in the hope of having a publicly traded company that would manage a significant amount of care in this country. PHYCOR was a failure, as were most of the PPMCs that attempted to do the same thing. In 1998 there were over a hundred private and public companies applying this business model, and today there are just a couple of them left.

Physicals* & Wellness Visits

Camp, Sports, & Annual School Physicals - ages 21 and under	$39.00** (usually $60)
Administrative Physicals College & Trade School Physicals Child Care, Senior Care & Healthcare Provider Physicals Driver's License Physicals Employment License Physicals Employment Physicals Professional Licensure Physicals Premarital Physicals	$69.00
Medicare Wellness Visits	$0†

Figure 20.1 Walgreens has adopted total price transparency which includes a very straightforward cost for a Medicare Wellness Visit – $0.

markets for additional capital, at least until the markets figured out that they had no real business case.

While the hospital looks at the enterprise with its physicians as a source of referrals, the physician looks at the enterprise, in whatever form it takes, as a source of continued capital and a partner that is flush with resources and talent. Sadly, both the institutions and the physicians are naïve.

All parties need to develop realistic measures for financial success and sustainability, and they have to look at a 3- to 4-year planning horizon for the mutual investment. In this time frame, the success will be dictated by how fast the markets in which they are operating mature. In this sense, maturity means how quickly alternative payment and reimbursement strategies become the norm. None of the developments referenced in this book would be initiated without the pressures of the Patient Protection and Affordable Care Act (PPACA), insurance exchanges, consumer choice, and capitated pricing. These new challenges are best referenced by a placard from a Walgreens web-based source that contains direct consumer pricing (Figure 20.1).* No need to negotiate.

This reflects the consumer pricing option against which the health care enterprise has to compete. But it is not just price—Walgreen's offers convenience, parking, and complementary shopping. It also has a pharmacy on site as well as any kind of DME† necessary to support the standard patient experience.

A planning model has to be developed that embraces change and transformation built from components that include infrastructure, finances, and the consumer part of the demand equation. Once the plan is agreed upon, it must be constantly updated and improved upon given the additional knowledge that only market development can provide.

Do we have a plan that is flexible?

* Walgreens Prevention and Wellness Menu, http://takecarehealth.com/Cost_Menu.aspx.

† DME is for durable medical equipment, which includes health care supplies and appliances.

Do we have internal indicators that trigger action?
Are we prepared to act decisively to change course or direction when necessary?
Are we achieving any of our projections?
What new initiatives in the marketplace should inform our judgment now?

There is a saying in Catholic-sponsored health care circles that the sponsored systems are always in the best product lines and always have a full range of business services, but they are the last to go into the ones that are profitable and the last to get out of the ones that aren't. Actually, the Catholic-sponsored groups are not alone in this first-last conundrum. Most health systems have a major issue with timing and the deployment of resources.

Business development for any of the organizations referenced in this book should have the following characteristics:

- A defined market arena in which it operates
- Sufficient capital to stay the course through a 3- to 4-year transition
- A strike team that can respond quickly to market opportunities
- A link to the balance sheet and income statement of a major health care resource that can back its development efforts—and act as a backer for any arrangements necessary for risk pools (capitation)
- An administrative team that has a background in private companies and corporate development
- An infrastructure equal to or better than that of the firms against which they are bidding—or with which they are contracting
- A physician governance process that can add value to the contracting and fulfillment equation

Summary Issues

- Markets are changing faster than planners can keep up.
- An organization needs staying power (capital) and a will to use it.
- The development team and the organization for which it is working will need to have flexibility and the ability to make decisions quickly. If there is a solid plan backing the team, this will not be a problem.
- If the market shifts, the organization must be able to reflect on that shift and either move with it very quickly or, alternatively, elect to stay the course and resist any change that might not complement its overall vision.

Chapter 21

To Understand Success, Study Failure

In the 1980s, subcapitation* appeared as an option, and in some markets as the only option, for doctors and specialists and health care systems. Now that most operators have forgotten the lessons learned in the 1980s, it is back, in the form of accountable care organizations (ACOs) and a variety of population management risk contracts and payment schemes.

For some practices, it might work this time, if it is approached with purpose and with physicians who have their motivation aligned with the goals of the health care system in some form of compensation that is not fee for service based. What are the signals that an organization failed, or is about to fail, or is positioning itself for failure? There are certainly some elements that are common—the practice acquisitions are generally understaffed at the administrative level, and they are undermanaged by any measure of talent and experience. The practices that have been acquired do not have the necessary infrastructure in place to handle capitation, quality, or efficiency measures. The practices are populated with doctors who are from a generation that grew into medicine and into their medical careers chasing fee-for-service and procedural revenues.

* Subcapitation is the alternative to fee-for-service payments through which a payer (an insurance company or Medicaid or Medicare) will pay a group for some component of care for a group of patients. This transfers the risk from the payer to the provider.

The Group in Crisis

Actually, most medical groups are in a state of constant tension that borders on crisis, if not chaos. The challenge of a medical group that is in change or transition can bring issues that have been long-standing problems to the forefront as major issues. Also, the change in a leadership or governance or management structure will allow issues that have been long simmering to surface in a rapid boil state. It seems trivial to compare something like the deconstruction of the Soviet Union and the resulting disorder in the Balkan States to a medical staff transformation, but the change from a dictatorial style of entrepreneurial management to one that is more bureaucratic and, in some cases, participatory (democratic?) allows long-standing issues to come to the forefront. These can be major items or minor matters, but when they all surface at once, the result can be challenging. Challenges can be handled. Catastrophic challenges have to be handled in crisis mode.

The administrator charged with the direct management of the practice has to reflect on the continued role of the physician in the direct delivery of care and in the overall leadership position in the practice as the issues that are emerging are categorized and addressed. The Kettering* comment goes something like this: "A problem that can be defined is already half solved." Many times there are many problems, and the challenge is to define them and define the stakeholders that have to be included in their solution. In a crisis situation or a turnaround, the manager should move quickly to (1) assess the situation, (2) define the stakeholders, and (3) prepare an "issues listing" that can be used to prioritize problems and actions to resolve them.

The use of an issues listing as a tool for discussion is one that is employed by consultants who, quite frankly, often do not have a grasp on the situation and who are struggling to gain ascendancy and credibility in a group that is unstructured.†

Developing an Emergency Turnaround Strategy

Sometimes it is helpful to check a laundry list of activities just to see if all the bases are covered. In an ambulatory setting there is a certain set of building blocks that comprise a successful practice. This is a listing of the basics. It is not meant to replace the need for a formal business plan that might be used in a calm and reasoned environment. The intent is to use a list like this to ask basic questions about

* Charles Franklin Kettering (1876–1958), American inventor and social philosopher. Kettering was a contemporary of Alfred P. Sloan and worked as a developer and innovator at General Motors during its formative years.

† There is no source for this statement, except for my own experience. I have been a consultant for over 25 years and can attest to this struggle and the challenge of moving a group from problem definition to resolution. Many times, the problems are actually resolved by airing the definitions and scope.

the general marketing position of the practice and to try to understand what is missing. Any business consultant will judge a business, first and foremost, by top-end revenue. Top-end revenue in a practice is related to patients, and the patients are derived from basic channels of service, access, and promotion.

If the practice is in a crisis situation, have these bases been covered? Of course, none of these items can be taken out of context. We need to agree on the basic focus of the practice unit and who the practice is supposed to serve. What is the practice able to offer this group as a basic value proposition? If this practice were in a successful state, what would it look like?

However, the vision and the plan pale when there is a financial crisis and the practice or the enterprise is in trouble, in a free fall or a tailspin, or whatever jargon applies. Hopefully, the following process can be applied in time to stem the bleeding.

Immediately:

- Communicate the severity of the situation along with a sense of urgency.
- Put a moratorium on all on new hires, or replacement hires, on all travel and conferences, on overtime, and on new capital purchases.
- Cease any consulting agreements or locums coverage.
- Announce the pay cuts and sacrifices that top management will be taking as they lead the internal team on a rescue effort.

Establish an efficiency/responsibility task force to oversee progress and do the following near term:

- Assign physicians to the team for oversight of patient care issues.
- Address revenue recovery (collections).
- Drop any nonprofitable offices or service lines.
- Address all vendor contracts from most costly on down.
- Renegotiate all contracts with managed care plans.

There are standards for longer-term and intermediate-term efforts, but they are things that should be done in any case. Recognize an emergency for what it is—a market misstep, a misfit on a program, a misalignment of incentives. Short-term and immediate cost containment will not be the answer when millions of dollars are on the line. Physician and provider contracts are multiyear in length, and the idea of completely revamping the whole structure should be considered when the first waves of panic start to make themselves felt from the CFO's office.

Properly timed and implemented effectively, the transition from independent operators to an integrated team can be hazardous. If the timing is off and the contracting is term fixed (for doctors) when the markets are moving rapidly from traditional to risk oriented, the results can be immediate and the scale of losses can be consequential. Longer-term responses will need to be considered, such as an overhaul of all budget assumptions and consolidation of offices. The successful turnaround may encompass divestiture of some clinic operations and rebasing some physician and provider contracts. All of this is painful, but one has to remember that hospitals now are going bankrupt and, in some cases, going down in bankruptcy for the second time.*

These are some of the basic marketing and service issues that should be addressed to define whether the practice is achieving some level of market position.

The Group Approaching Crisis

Fire blowing out the windows of a building is quite different from a smoke alarm. However, when early signs of failure or, if not failure, the inability to make objectives or meet goals is evident, management should still move fast. What are these signs? Generally, failing to negotiate a good contract or a couple of bad quarters of performance on an otherwise good contract would make investors take up a position near a doorway. However, when managers and doctors are invested at the level of their personal income stream, there is more at stake and they have a tendency to wait out the bad quarter or the bad contract by hoping (with no apparent reason) that it is an anomaly or something that can be "managed through."

The challenge of dampened revenue in health care, with longer-term contracts and embedded capital, cannot be corrected by laying off a couple of medical assistants. The practices have economic scalability only on an upward slope, and then only with some difficulty. A brace of practices or a group of practices do not have a way to downscale efficiently. Health care is not a factory, and the microeconomic models show scale adjustments only in theory. Figure 21.1 shows the typical cost levels of a practice. Everything in the zone that is outlined, where the practice moves from 4,000 to 6,500 encounters, is moving at once—the need for more staff driving the need for more room (capital). Painful on the upside, and once capital is applied in a new building, the fixed costs are established for the long term.

If the enterprise misses a mark on patient enrollment or loses a contract, there is no way to scale back easily. The choices are limited to divestiture, joint venture with another provider, merger, or reassessment of the organization's basic business case. There may be a short time between realizing that there is need for change and determining which changes to make, and the management team is well advised to always have contingency plans in hand for unexpected strategic events.

---

* St. Vincent's New York actually went down twice. Talent and money could not overcome the pressures on this proud institution, and its medical services to the community have been replaced by an urgent care center and an ambulance service to take inpatient admissions uptown to Lenox Hill.

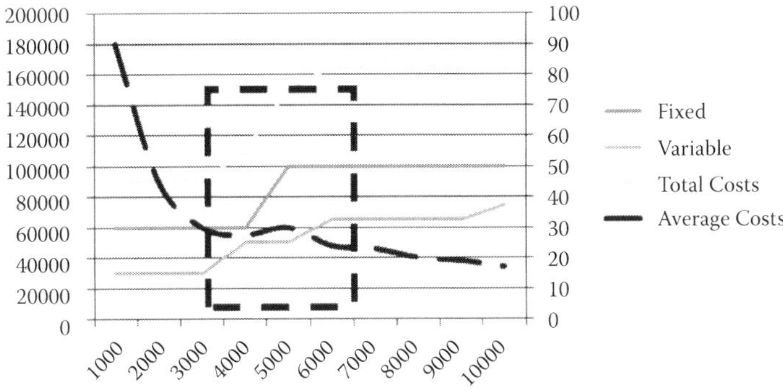

Figure 21.1 The microeconomics of physician practices presents real challenges for owner/managers.

Summary Issues

- Contingencies should be planned in advance. Early warning signals should put the staff and the doctors on notice immediately and prompt actions that can preserve the enterprise.
- Drastic action for a health care group would be considered standard for a business. This includes downsizing, divesting, rethinking assumptions, and abandoning product lines. The goal is to emerge stronger and leaner and maybe in a different part of the market.
- Financial planning should be benchmarked on a monthly basis and gross process indicators—new patients, patient visits, cash deposits, days in AR, etc.—should be monitored even more frequently.

Appendix: Samples and Examples

Sample: Practice Manager Job Description (Director Level)

Position title: Executive Director, Physician Program Development
Department: Administration
Reports to: VP Network Development
Position summary:

Leads the strategic planning process for all physician practice development activities; assures that strategic plan is implemented fully in accordance with established timelines for each project and priority position within the plan.

Monitors financial and operational performance of each site, service, and practice per operating and capital budgets and established goals.

Supervises the performance of the individual practice administrators; acts as liaison between system administrative/support staff and practice management and physicians.

Reviews all contracts, loans, capital equipment requests, etc.

Minimal qualifications for position:
Bachelor's degree in business administration, finance, or health care-related field required; master's degree preferred. Minimum 10 years of experience in health care, with focus on physician practice management or outpatient hospital department operations. Demonstrated expertise in working with physicians, preparing budgets, business plan development and financial analyses, and personnel management.

Essential position elements:

- Interviews, hires, and monitors performance of all practice administrative staff.
- Reviews all budgets, capital, and operating; signs off on same before submission to finance committee or other advisory bodies.

- Chairs strategic planning committee for all physician practice development activities. Assures that plans are documented, prioritized, staffed, and funded.
- Coordinates the preparation of monthly financial and operational reports regarding each site, each service for all physician practices. Identifies problem areas and prepares recommendations for corrective actions when necessary.
  - In reporting financial, volume, and other statistical data, develops and maintains a format to allow a consolidated balance sheet and income statement approach where appropriate.
  - Assures that financial reporting and accounting methods are consistent with those of private practices generally.
  - Assures that a cost accounting system is developed that allows site-specific financial management in accordance with approved budget.
- Assists in the development of physician and vendor contracts. Assures that compensation plans for physicians are competitive and financially feasible.
- Acts as liaison between support staff and practice management team and physicians.
- Assures that problems are identified and resolved in order to allow efficient and cost-effective operations; removes barriers at the practice level that impede progress in achieving goals (financial and performance). In this role, advises the following administrative departments in policies and procedures that will enhance (or impede) development:
  - Finance
  - Purchasing
  - Human resources
  - Medical staff
- Reviews all practice-related policies, procedures, benefit plans, etc. Assures that consistency from practice to practice is created whenever feasible, and that wages, salaries, and benefit plans are competitive with those of private physician offices in the area.
- Coordinates services to achieve goals established for the practices and vice versa. Develops new programs and services that support these goals.
- Assists in negotiations with large groups, significant vendor contracts, etc.
- Addresses all aspects of compliance and regulatory standards to assure that the organization has minimal risk or exposure to any matter that might be deemed inappropriate by a regulatory agency.

Model: The Definition of Citizenship and a Bonus Policy to Recognize It

The award for citizenship is based on a pass/fail test. As an example, three documented complaints, fouls, errors, events, or whatever, trigger a loss of this component of the bonus. The idea is that a practitioner that is "high maintenance" will be defined by the number of times that he or she will cause the practice and the administration of the practice to address his or her behavior in a formal fashion. The NBA uses a "foul out" process that assumes that the referees would make a determination on any particular foul that might be open to discussion, but that four fouls simply would indicate that the recipient of that many calls simply needs to be out of the game.

The amount to be placed in the citizenship category is determined annually by some level of the governance process that includes physicians. The criteria for earning (or failing to earn) the citizenship allotment is based upon the physician's compliance to standards defined by the same group so that all the stakeholders are in the same collaborative space. Good citizenship and appropriate team contributions are assumed. The award is something that is not earned but lost.

Some examples that physicians might agree would produce a foul include:

Failing to maintain timely charting causing repeated administrative reminders or temporary suspension of privileges.

Failure to maintain a schedule resulting in other cases or other schedules to have to be modified to account for the physician behavior pattern.

Failure to cover call as demonstrated by the need for staff to pursue alternate physicians for patient services after attempting to reach the doctor on call.

Failure to complete medical reports causing coding and billing staff to fall behind in the processing of patient claims.

Failure to maintain proper decorum and interpersonal relationships on a professional level resulting in complaints to HR or the medical staff office or to the practice that need to be adjudicated in some way by administration.

Failure to support accreditation and credentialing processes by not meeting basic criteria for licensure and continuing medical education (CME) standards.

Failure to attend regularly scheduled meetings causing staff follow-up either for gaining required input or for separate and individual coaching on matters that were covered in a general session.

All of these are examples. They are easily documented since each lapse by the doctor is something that creates some other event and a cost for the practice, for physician colleagues, for other professionals. The norm is that none of these behaviors are routine and there is no need, if the policy is properly written to have the citizenship program overseen by any one medical director or administrator. The doctors agree on what a lapse might be, and at the end of the year, the physician files are either clear of any follow-up reporting or variances or have something like three or more instances, which would be an indication to withhold "citizenship pool" dollars.

The pool dollars become reallocated among the other providers, or they can be moved to the next revenue and income cycle. This is not supposed to be a process by which some doctors gain from the behavior of other physicians. Everyone is supposed to be a "winner" in this category, except someone who has egregious behavior. An additional comment is that there is no appeals process. If this were based on one instance, there would be an appeal. This program is based upon multiple events. There is no apportionment of the award—all or nothing.

Sample: A Physician Letter of Hire

Dear Doctor _____________:

Thank you for participating in our selection process for a full-time internist to serve the patients of Chickaming General Receiving Hospital. This communication is a formal offer to you for full-time employment. This position will be structured through the practice association that is sponsored by the hospital. Subject to the verification of your credentials and your acceptance of a final contract form, we offer you the following employment package.

The position for which you are being hired is that of a full-time clinical internist employed by Practice Partners LLC (a division of the hospital), to be based primarily at Celery Corners and other locations, to be determined collaboratively. Your time will be equally apportioned between these assignments, except as otherwise detailed in this communication.

Office space and support staff will be provided for you at the sites of assignment.

The position will be compensated at the base salary level of $175,000 per year, paid in equal biweekly segments.

As a condition of employment, you must maintain full admitting privileges at the hospital(s) to which you are assigned.

The term of the contract will be for 1 year, beginning immediately. The terms of a renewal clause after the first year of employment will be described in the final contract. There is a bonus contemplated that will be described in the contract, which will be based upon a combination of performance and production. The bonus is entirely associated with your efforts, and it will not be linked to overall system performance in any way. Because of the production nature of the bonus, it is not guaranteed, except if you meet the standards that will be specified in the final contract.

Your duties will include the provision of clinical services generally coordinated through the existing Department of Medicine of the hospital and medical support to the practice sites at which you will be assigned.

The position will also require a call and duty schedule that will be designed on an equitable basis with the other physicians in your call rotation who provide similar services. This schedule will be published quarterly throughout the year.

You may be asked, from time to time, to participate in scheduled teaching events and in general hospital rounding. The work week will be structured as 4 days weekly, or 8 half-day sessions, for scheduled office hours caring for the needs of the ambulatory and inpatient population, with an additional business day assigned for procedures or other duties as might complement a medical practice. This definition is not meant or intended to describe, define, or limit the hourly commitment, but to specify the minimum amount of scheduled session time that is expected.

The position will allow for 3 weeks of paid annual vacation, after the first 6 months of full-time employment. An additional 3 days will be allowed annually for preapproved CME. Standard holidays will also be paid in conjunction with those that are traditionally recognized in the local area. These will be compensated by the allowance of paid time off when the holiday falls on a scheduled office session, not through additional compensation.

The practice will cover costs associated with CME, travel associated with CME, dues, periodicals, license fees, memberships, etc., up to a level of $3,000 per year.

Your clinical work will be supervised by the administrator of clinical programming, and medical oversight will be coordinated by the chief of medicine. On an administrative and operational basis, you will be working with the practice administrative team.

Your benefits will include health insurance, life insurance, holiday pay, workers' compensation coverage, and all other benefits that are routinely covered by the hospital for similar positions. These benefits do include employee participation in certain premium levels, depending upon the level of benefits elected.

The contract you will be offered will include provisions for malpractice coverage. Qualifying for standard malpractice rates is a requirement of this offer. You will be expected to join the Chickaming Physician Hospital Network (a managed care contracting organization) and maintain provider status with all of the managed care programs sanctioned by this network. The contract will contain a standard restrictive covenant and noncompete clause. These clauses will incorporate a requirement that your medical staff privileges will be co-terminal with your contract.

Upon signing of the contract, we will advance you a sum of $10,000 that you may use for relocation and resettlement purposes. This must be repaid over the first 6 months of the contract, except for any amount that is directly related to fees associated with a licensed moving and transport service.

We hope that this offer meets your needs and reflects your understanding of the position as it was described. Everyone with whom I have discussed your candidacy is eager to hear that you are committed to joining the staff.

Because of the nature of the local medical job market and the need to address the patients in our community, we can hold this position open only for a term of 14 days after your receipt of this letter. After that point in time, we would still welcome your interest, but in the interest of our patients and our programming, we must continue to interview candidates.

We certainly hope to hear from you soon. If you have questions, please do not hesitate to contact me. If you accept the basic terms of this agreement, please sign the bottom of the letter and return it to me by fax at _____________, or indicate your acceptance by return e-mail. Upon receipt, we will immediately begin the preparation of your contract.

[This is a pretty standard document, but it is one that contains almost all of the points that a hospital or health system might make in an offer. The candidate would be expected to challenge the salary, bonus provisions, terms of the contract, and other ambiguous areas.]

Sample: Noncompete/Restrictive Covenant with Liquidated Damages

The inclusion of noncompete clauses and nonsolicitation clauses and restrictive covenants is important in order to maintain practice resources that have been acquired in a competitive environment and at what are certainly nontrivial costs. They should be specific to a reasonable geographic service area to a time limit and to the specific type of activity that is being addressed. In order to have the most impact, they should be structured with a specified amount that both parties agree upon as liquidated damages.

The questions that should be asked of counsel include their understanding of what should be reasonable as far as the determination of distance and time and what the history is concerning the enforcement of clauses of this nature. However, the reason to include some level of specific monetary damages is that this makes the agreement more enforceable and less likely to be interpreted by a court as lacking in prenegotiated definition.

The following language is an example of the type of agreement that should be considered as part of most physician contracts.

During the term of this agreement and for a period of 2 years from the effective date of the termination hereof (the "restrictive covenant period"), EMPLOYEE shall not, without the written consent of the CORPORATION, engage directly or indirectly, as a principal, agent, employee, partner, shareholder, investor, staff member, consultant, or otherwise, in a private practice of [type of practice] within the counties of [name of county], nor shall EMPLOYEE directly or indirectly solicit in any manner any individuals who are then or who had been patients of the CORPORATION during the term of this agreement.

The PARTIES acknowledge that in the event EMPLOYEE breaches any of the provisions of this paragraph, then the CORPORATION'S damages shall be difficult to measure, and the CORPORATION is entitled to a payment for liquidated damages, and not as a penalty, the sum of $2,500.00 per day. It is agreed that in the event EMPLOYEE breaches any of the provisions of this paragraph, the CORPORATION may apply to any court of competent jurisdiction to enjoin any violation hereof, threatened or actual.

The covenants contained in this paragraph are intended to be separate and divisible covenants, and if, for any reason, any one or more of them shall be held to be invalid or unenforceable, in whole or in part, it is agreed that same shall not be held to affect the validity or enforceability of any other such covenant of this agreement. The terms, period, and damages set forth in this paragraph shall be reduced to the maximum terms, damages, and periods permitted by law, if necessary, in order to uphold the validity of this paragraph.

Discussion: Call Compensation

Should "call" even be considered for physician compensation models? It all depends—can coverage be assured if it is not? More often, with aging medical staffs and hired doctors, the answer is no.

1. Physicians in many specialties might be legitimately paid for "availability," for providing uncompensated care to service patients referred through the emergency department (ED), and for support for training programs and staff house officers.
2. The payment structure should address the issue of duplicate pay for service time and assure that physicians do not receive payment for on-call services when the clinical services that they provide during that period might be reimbursed by patients, other payers, or other sponsoring entities.
3. Compensation, logically, requires that specific and identifiable services are provided. These services might include, but are not limited to, the following:
   a. Participation in an ongoing, defined call rotation that requires coverage of a service or some form of defined availability.
   b. Provision of consultative services to patients treated during the on-call service.
   c. Response to call according to established facility standards and medical staff requirements.
   d. Cooperation with care management, risk management, and quality initiatives.
   e. Completion of all required documentation.
   f. Support of hospital-sponsored teaching programs, when indicated, for call-related patient encounters.
4. Provision of adequate patient follow-up for patients who originate from a call event regardless of their ability to pay.
5. Call pay should only be supported by the provision of actual and necessary services that may not otherwise be compensated.
6. Opportunity to participate in call should be offered equally to all eligible and interested participating physicians.
7. Scheduling of call shift should be governed by written operational procedures to ensure fairness for all interested parties.
8. In developing a call-pay methodology, the institution should enforce a system that is organized to collect and quantify process measures that can be used to confirm and correct any proxy standards that might have been applied in developing initial contract terms.

The *Physician On-Call Pay Survey Report 2011*, prepared by Sullivan, Cotter and Associates, Inc., reported that 63% of hospital survey participants have experienced difficulty finding physicians to provide call coverage,[*] and that the most common form of on-call compensation for physicians is a stipend or hourly rate.[†] Even though there are a number of surveys available for reports on call pay, there are none that are statistically significant or which detail local call rates. Consultants and administrator should apply a compilation of available market data and an application of locally derived assumptions based upon the consideration of the proposed financial relationship in its entirety before proceeding with a pay-for-call program.

[*] Page 12.
[†] Page 13.

Revenue Management Standards

Revenue is something that needs to be analyzed and managed like any other practice resource. It depends upon the number of patients who come through the door of a practice and also the mix of procedures or services done for the patients and the payer mix, which reflects the reimbursement support of the patients. Usually, getting more money into a practice does not merely mean doing more, but it may mean doing different things for a different mix of patients and billing them all on an optimal level. Registration, coding, collection, and follow-up are key to the success of this effort, and regular and timely reporting is a must for a successful practitioner.

The following questions may assist in the analysis:

1. Do we know what is being done and for whom? Are we aware of our patient mix, and at the end of the day, do we audit the registration or charge slips to be sure that we have captured all of the services that have been provided? Do we have an idea what each physician is charging for what he or she actually does? Is there an audit trail that ties back to scheduling?
2. This is a function of not only registration, but also auditing the physicians' behavior.
3. Are we charging for all consults? Are we charging for all physician visits not in the office—hospital visits?
4. Are we logging activities that may not have a charge, but which reflect key elements of physician service? Telephone consults? Meetings? Courtesy and social patient visits?
5. If we do something, is it charged? Do we have a tracking to see that all of the slips or charges get to some sort of billing point? Again, is there an audit trail?
6. Are we charging the optimal amount for each service? How often is coding reviewed? Is there an effective use of modifiers?
7. If the charges are registered, at the optimal amount, are they actually billed? Are they billed in a timely fashion? Are we taking advantage of timing with respect to electronic billing? Are we billing procedures of more expensive services sooner (same day)? Again, where is the audit trail to reflect the timing of the billing function—from service to transmission?
8. Are we billing it right the first time? Are the codes and the background information appropriate? Is the documentation appropriate? If we bill at the appropriate rate, and it is properly coded, is the payment appropriate? Do we assume that the payers pay at the proper level, and do we challenge their assumptions about the amounts that they pay? They audit us—do we audit them? There should be a functions-specific and a person-specific log of quality or effectiveness (or reject status) to assist in monitoring this process.
9. If we are billing, and if third-party payment is appropriate, is the co-payment or deductible collected?

10. If procedures are billed and a third party rejects payment, is the rejection inquiry answered in a timely fashion? Is the patient informed of the rejection? Is the billing modified or appealed? How is this tracked and reported? What is the feedback loop for reducing this rate of rejection?
11. If payment is not received from the third party, and if co-payment or deductibles are not collected at the time of visit, does the patient receive a bill in a timely fashion? Is the bill correct? Are the results of our collection efforts efficient? Does the patient billing cycle get monitored independently of payer cycles?
12. If we are unsuccessful in collecting, is there an analysis to see what has been done with respect to the process that could improve this ratio? Are we writing off things in an appropriate fashion?
13. If we see a patient (or have experience with a provider or payer) who is consistently delinquent, are we reevaluating our relationship with him or her?
14. Do we have a rationale for accepting assignment or not accepting assignment?
15. Do we have a rationale, protocol, or policy for determining whether or not a charge should be written off or whether a bill should be reduced in a special case of some sort?
16. Do we audit our own processes on a regular basis so that we learn from our mistakes and our errors? Do we have and use benchmarks? Do we exceed the norm and are we on a continuous improvement cycle relative to internal markers?
17. Are there opportunities for nontraditional sources of revenue (capitation, bonuses, case rates, whatever)?
18. Is the charge master up to date and updated regularly?

Policy: Physician Practice Purchases for Health Care Institutions

Every institution that has a process of buying practices should coordinate that process through a single administrative structure and under a program that is coordinated with executives from finance and from the compliance area. There should be a set of policies to guarantee that the process conforms to standards that meet regulatory guidelines and which achieve parity internal to the organization. The following policy is offered as a guide:

Purpose: To assure that all practices acquired by the institution are evaluated using standard evaluation methodologies, and that offers prepared for physicians are consistent with parameters established by the administration and the board and are in line with compliance guidelines.

The following process should be followed by staff working with physician recruitment that is related to practice purchases.

The initial step in evaluating any practice for purchase by __________ will be a meeting with the physician owner and a representative of __________. At that meeting, various options regarding acquisition will be discussed, the timeline for practice evaluation reviewed, and the interest level of the physician in acquisition and employment by __________ assessed.

Following the initial meeting with the physician, should he or she express serious interest in acquisition and employment opportunities at __________, a formal letter of intent will be generated that outlines the process in writing for the practice evaluation indicating a timeline under which the process will be completed and signed by the appropriate administrative staff member at __________.

A copy of the standard letter of intent is attached to this policy as Attachment A.

Practice financial evaluation:

1. Document request. The standard document request form will be enclosed with the letter of intent. This form includes a request for tax returns, productivity reports based on billing system information, a listing of employees by job title and salary information, etc. The standard document request form is attached to this policy as Attachment B.
2. Financial analysis. Once all of the requested information has been received from the individual practice, __________ financial analyst will begin to review the documents and develop standardized spreadsheets. These spreadsheets will include all of the following: historical income and expense spreadsheet.

   This spreadsheet will be developed using historical income and expense statements for a minimum of the past 3 fiscal years and the practice tax returns for the same periods. If the physician is a sole proprietor, the tax return and Schedule C's will be evaluated.

The spreadsheet developed will include, at a minimum, the reporting of personnel-related expenses, building repairs and maintenance, administrative costs, and supply costs as separate categories. In addition, a category characterized as "physician residual" will be isolated to include all expenses directly attributable to the providers in the practice historically. This will include the following expense items:

Physician salary
Employer payroll tax contribution (if a professional corporation exists)
Pension and profit sharing contribution for the physician providers
Health, life, and disability insurance expenses for the physician providers
Auto expenses
Travel expenses
Continuing medical education expenses
Malpractice expenses
Any and all other expenses directly attributable to any physician provider

3. Personnel budget. Using historical information, a 1-year personnel historical budget will be prepared and compared to the total expense reported on the tax returns. This budget will include the staff member's date of hire, title, licensure status, if any, average number of hours routinely scheduled to work each week, and hourly rate. In addition, a 3-year projection of future personnel-related costs will be prepared using __________ actual salaries and benefits costs as developed and available.
4. Building repairs and maintenance. A budget will be prepared for rent, maintenance, and equipment expenses, as appropriate. Should the physician own the space in which he or she works, a standardized lease will be offered to the physician at market rates for the space being utilized. In no case will __________ pay above market rates for property to physicians. It is, likewise, not the policy of __________ at this time to acquire real estate as an asset.
5. Production. If accurate records are available from the physician's private office billing system, a historical accounting of procedural volume by Current Procedural Terminology (CPT) code for the prior 2 fiscal years will be produced. This will allow an analysis of each provider's productivity over that period of time in relative value units using the currently approved Health Care Financing Administration resource-based relative value system as published from time to time in the Federal Register.
6. Operating *pro forma*. Using the historical income and expense spreadsheet produced previously, staff will prepare a 3-year projection of income and expenses using standard inflation factors for medical and nonmedical goods and services (per the Department of Labor, Bureau of Statistics) for the region. Also taken into account in this process will be unusual expense items

historically and actual expenses as projected under the __________ umbrella for the future. These actual numbers will include the salaries and benefits costs for all employees and physicians, as well as malpractice rates as part of the __________ policy. The initial purchase price for the assets of the practice will be amortized over the 3-year period of the projection without any cost of money imputed. The operating *pro forma* will reflect, on a cash basis, the projected operating income/(loss) of the practice.

7. Site visit. In addition to the preparation of the operating *pro forma* and related spreadsheets, an actual site visit will be performed by __________ staff to evaluate various aspects of the practice and the site. This analysis will be performed in a standardized fashion using forms prepared for that purpose. The assets valuation will be a part of the site visit. The site inspection will include all of the following:
   a. Medical records, quality and count: Staff will attempt to estimate the number of active medical records in the practice. For the purposes of the practice evaluation, an active medical record is considered to be one for any patient who has been seen by a provider in the practice within the last 36 months. In addition, the medical records will be reviewed at random and a checklist will be completed that attempts to assess the quality of the medical records documentation. A copy of the standard checklist is attached to this policy as Attachment C.
   b. There will be prepared, at the site visit or in conjunction with the physician's office staff, a comprehensive listing of capital equipment. The capital equipment will be valued by __________ staff members using comparables from prior practice evaluations. Should it be determined that an outside third-party appraisal is to be done, a firm will be chosen and approval will be obtained from appropriate __________ administrative staff members to contract for these services. The approximate cost for a typical one-physician practice outside appraisal is $3,000.00.
   c. Billing policies and procedures: A standardized questionnaire will be reviewed with billing staff members to assess the manner in which cash is handled, patient bills and insurance claims are generated, and accounts receivable are collected. A written assessment of this procedure will be included with the final site inspection report.

Practice acquisition offer:

Subsequent to the preparation of the operating *pro forma* and the site inspection of the practice, utilizing all information obtained in the course of these two processes, __________ staff will prepare a practice description and narrative notes that describe the practice in general and also review any unusual expenses or circumstances that should be brought to the attention of __________ administrative staff members. The assumptions used in projecting future expenses will likewise be referred to in this document. An example of the narrative practice description and supporting notes is attached to the policy as Attachment D.

Employment agreement:
Using the physician's historical actual salary as a base, __________ staff will attempt to estimate the physician's salary in the future as a __________ employee. A final offer will be prepared as a summary of the financial aspects of the practice acquisition and the employment agreement for the physician. This offer will include the physician's first-year base salary, his or her continuing medical education benefits allowance, his or her signing bonus, the payment for his or her assets including the restrictive covenant, the furniture, fixtures, and equipment, and the medical records. An estimate of the value of the physician's benefits for such things as health insurance, life insurance, disability insurance, pension, and profit sharing contribution will likewise be incorporated in this document. A sample offer document is attached to this policy as Attachment E.

Presentation of offer to physician:
Once the offer has been reviewed and approved by __________ staff, the staff will arrange for a personal meeting with the physician to present the offer to him or her formally. The offer will be reviewed in detail with the physician personally and a copy of the offer left with him or her for review. In addition, copies of the proposed assets purchase agreement and the employment agreement will be left for the physician's perusal and the advice of the physician's legal counsel. A deadline will be given in writing at which time the physician will be expected to respond to the offer. The deadline should not be more than 30 days following the presentation of the offer.

Summary:
The practice valuation methodology being described in this policy is not to be construed as the future stream of income approach to practice valuation, nor does it include the valuation of the business as an ongoing concern with a component for goodwill. The practice methodology being utilized by __________ is purely an asset purchase methodology with the opportunity for the physician to become an employee of __________. The due diligence performed by staff in the course of the practice valuation is limited to an attempt to display, as accurately as possible, the past 3 years' historical actual revenue and expense. This is based upon financial documents received from the practice, including tax returns. Wherever expenses or revenue seem unusual with regard to what might be expected, further documentation will be pursued. An effort will likewise be made to identify any income received but not reported on the tax return, and any expenses not associated with the business that were reported on the tax return. This will be done in an effort to more accurately project future income and expenses under __________.

__________ staff will not be performing uniform commercial code searches with respect to debt, nor will they be assessing the malpractice history of the practitioner involved, except that any information they become apprised of will be made known to appropriate __________ administrative staff members and attorneys. Neither will staff be reviewing leases or other legal documents for assignability or potential problems. Those processes requiring additional expertise will be referred to the appropriate [health system] department.

Model: Physician Interview Tool

If you want to know what physicians like and do not like, ask them. However, use a survey process carefully. Surveying implies a dialogue, and asking a question about processes implies that there is interest in the answer. The mere initiation of a survey process will create the expectation that there will be two results: a report on the responses and action to fix whatever those surveyed feel might be broken. Don't survey doctors unless there is an intent to have definitive and focused follow-up.

If you do a survey, make it meaningful. This form is suggested since it is one that has a number of questions that are asked in a rather probing fashion. This is a useful tool since it goes far beyond most survey instruments. It can be modified in any way that seems to suit the situation, but there are some general guidelines that might be useful as background.

The reader will probably realize that this is a discussion survey that is best held with an outside and uninvolved third party. Also, the person conducting the survey should have some level of basic understanding of the situation in which the physician is operating and a degree of credibility with the doctor. Often, this may mean that a consultant is used for gathering the material, or if it is a large health care system, it can be a loaned executive from a partner hospital or from the corporate level of some organization that the physician recognizes to be independent. Common sense also dictates that a cluster of interviews be done in a constrained time period, and that the results are generalized or summarized before they are shared with administration or with the participants. The advantages of a survey process are probably evident. Done well, a lot of basic information and intelligence can be gained. However, done in a precipitous fashion outside of a basic planning structure, the survey itself can be demotivating since it will be effort expended on the part of the doctors and providers that is not followed by reciprocal action.

Another major mistake that surveyors might make is in gaining information that is quantified for every dimension except relevance. The responses from busy surgeons doing major cases in a surgery center should be weighted in a fashion that reflects their role and experience and commitment. New doctors with light case loads might report differently than the most senior and the busiest of the surgical staff. Their responses should not be weighted equally. A survey that misses just one important physician (the department chair, the busiest cardiologist, etc.) may actually be dismissed by the very stakeholders that need to support the processes that are intended to be the result of the survey effort.

The survey header should include basic registration information such as time, location, survey conditions, name of the surveyor, etc. One obvious note is that the survey is a process and the value is information, and each interview and interviewee is unique. Therefore, the process may be guided by individual interests, ideas, and passion as opposed to the questions in this guide. Background information for the interview should be available (organization charts, vision statements, planning calendar, etc.) and a general preamble should be delivered about confidentiality and openness. There is a preamble that is suggested as an "opener."

Given your understanding of this (planning? transition?) process, what is the area that you would most like to make sure we address first so that we have a full and complete understanding of your concerns prior to the end of this session (governance, operations, interinstitutional issues, administrative matters, income distribution, expansion issues, personnel?)?

We need to make sure that we are not only talking to the various physicians, but that we are giving appropriate weight to their opinions and input. If I could only talk with five or six of the doctors on this list (besides yourself), which ones would you direct me to see in order to get a representative and balanced idea of the issues facing the enterprise?

If you could be the czar of the group for a year, what matters would you immediately change and how would the group look once you had completed your reign? This assumes total autonomy and no input from others.

If you left this institution tomorrow, what would be the reason on your letter of resignation? What is the most compelling reason (dissatisfier) that you think might prompt one of your colleagues to leave?

Do you feel that you receive regular, concise, and useful reports on which decisions can be made? If not, how can the reports you get be improved? As a (principal/partner/physician), is there any kind of information or background material that you feel that you need, but do not have the ability to access?

What are the readability and reliability of the reports? Do you feel the material that you are getting is trustworthy? Is it distributed in a fashion that allows reflection and review?

What are the drivers that you see directly affecting your income in the next 3 to 4 years (assuming that operations and cost considerations are not under consideration)?

Do you have any concrete suggestions that might be used to improve operational processes (back office, billing, scheduling, collections, management services organization (MSO) functions, etc.)?

With respect to governance, do you feel that there is a need to address certain issues at the local (hospital) level, apart from the group in general? If so, what are those areas that must be defined at the hospital (or procedural unit or surgery area) in order to maintain harmony?

Can you reflect on the administrative processes that have been most beneficial for you and your colleagues over the last 3 years? What initiatives do you feel will have the most positive effect on you in the near-term future?

What mistakes can you point to in the last 3 years that should be memorialized in this planning process so that they are not repeated?

What issues related to governance and group management are most important to address in the near term? Which features of the governance process could be defined better (made more effective and efficient) from your perspective?

Generally speaking, if you wanted to achieve a higher income level, would you be inclined to refine the personnel complement at your site and work in a few more cases (or shifts or call slots) or would you want your workload to remain approximately the same?

What do you see as the *two or three main problems* that you and your colleagues are facing in the near term? Are these problems that you would be willing to assist in solving?

What do you see as the *two or three main opportunities* that the overall enterprise might capitalize upon in the near term?

[Likert* format] Can you give me a 1 to 5 numbered answer (1 being DISAGREE, 3 being NO OPINION, and 5 representing AGREE)?

Personally, my workload and call load are just about right.

I think I am treated fairly with respect to compensation and time schedule assignments.

I feel that I have a say in the governance process.

I am confident in the administration that we have in place.

I think we could do better with respect to overhead.

I think that we provide excellent quality of care at the site that I work.

I feel that there should be a mandatory retirement age for physicians.

I feel that ___________

[The survey should end with the restatement of the fact that this is an exercise in the collection of issues and that it is part of an overall planning process. There should be some estimate of time frame for the completion of the initial survey effort and for the way in which the information will be further processed. Preferably, the surveyor should be able to share a calendar with the doctor that outlines the process in a formal fashion.]

---

* This is a scale patterned after that proposed and used by University of Michigan psychologist Rensis Likert (1903–1981), who demonstrated that collection of information obtained in this fashion was more dependable than other formats.

Glossary

Glossary of Terms

Accountable care organization: An entity that has physician leadership and systems for measuring and impacting the effectiveness and efficiency of patient care. It is specifically referenced in the PPACA. It crosses a variety of provider settings and requires a high degree of health system integration between and among all levels of providers. Generally, it is rewarded, and under the PPACA, it will be exposed to risk for the health status of the populations it serves.

Benchmarking: The determination of optimal or best practices by comparing the process measures in a health care entity against other providers or, internally, against its own past measured performance in order to pursue continuous quality improvement.

Bundling: A form of reimbursement that combines institutional and professional charges and ancillaries into a single payment, including any preoperative and postoperative care. Bundled payment schemes generally include some provision for cases that become catastrophic.

Capitalization rate: Any divisor (usually expressed as a percentage) used to convert an income stream from several periods from some source into a singular value, generally thought of as the net present value of a stream of income.

Capitation: A reimbursement method that pays a provider a set price for providing medical services to a defined population for a defined set of services, regardless of service utilization. Providers must provide care by calculating the expected volume of referrals, the average cost, and their ability to control utilization.

Carve-out: A service that is separated from all insurance risk and is covered by a separate contract between the insurer and the vendor. An example might be lab services that are often contracted to outside labs like Quest.

Clinical benchmarking: A type of benchmarking utilized for continuous development and maintenance of quality health care. The measures are targeted patient-centered outcomes, and evidence-based benchmarks for best practices.

Commercial reasonableness: The Department of Health and Human Services has interpreted "commercially reasonable" to mean that an arrangement appears to be "a sensible, prudent business agreement, from the perspective of the particular parties involved, even in the absence of any potential referrals." The Stark II Phase II commentary also suggests that "an arrangement will be considered 'commercially reasonable' in the absence of referrals if the arrangement would make commercial sense if entered into by a reasonable entity of similar type and size and a reasonable physician of similar scope and specialty, even if there were no potential DHS referrals."

Comprehensive or "turnkey" model: This type of MSO provides a comprehensive array of services, including all of the nonclinical aspects of a practice's operations.

Cost of capital: The expected rate of return that the market requires in order to attract funds to a particular investment.

Direct-to-consumer medicine (retail medicine): Medical services that are driven solely by consumer demand, because almost all of these types of procedures are not covered by either private or governmental insurance.

Electronic health record (EHR): Electronically maintained patient health information, such as patient demographics, notes, medications, medical history, laboratory date, or medical reports, that is generated by one or more encounters in any care delivery setting.

Excess earnings: That amount of anticipated economic benefits that exceeds an appropriate rate of return on the value of a selected asset base (often net tangible assets) used to generate those anticipated economic benefits.

External benchmarking: Consists of several different subcategories of benchmarking and includes any interentity comparison.

Fair market value (FMV): As defined by Stark II Phase I for the purpose of scrutinizing transactions between health care professionals, FMV is "the value in arm's-length transactions, consistent with general market value," without taking into account any ability between parties to refer business to each other.

Financial benchmarking: A method of financial analysis that may be used to understand the operational and financial status of a health care organization. Financial benchmarking consists of three steps: (1) historical subject benchmarking, (2) benchmarking to industry norms, and (3) financial ratio analysis.

Fully integrated medical group (FIMG) model: The most integrated type of physician organization, it has the greatest contracting and market leverage. Information systems, management, and other administrative functions may be centralized so that the organization can efficiently act as a single entity.

Gain sharing: An arrangement under which a hospital gives physicians a share of the reduction in the hospital's costs attributable in whole or in part to the physicians' efforts.

Goodwill: That intangible asset arising as a result of name, reputation, customer loyalty, location, products, and similar factors not separately identified.

Independent practice association: An association of independent physicians who maintain their own private practices but have joined together to enter into an agreement to treat the plan's enrollees.

Independent practice association (IPA) model: A practice established by physicians who intend to maintain their independent practices but seek to offer their services to HMOs or other risk sharing MCOs on a collective basis.

Intangible assets: Nonphysical assets, such as franchises, trademarks, patents, copyrights, goodwill, equities, mineral rights, and securities and contracts (as distinguished from physical assets), that grant rights and privileges and have value for the owner.

Integrated delivery system (IDS) model: A group of legally affiliated organizations in which hospitals and physicians combine their assets, efforts, risks, and rewards in order to deliver comprehensive health care services to the community. The legally affiliated entities perform all strategic planning and payer contracting for the various interests.

Integrated delivery systems: Vertically integrated organizations that are frequently comprised of insurers alongside physician practices, hospitals, and other entities that provide medical care to a specific population.

Managed care organization (MCO): An organization that provides managed health care services.

Management services organization (MSO) model: The MSO typically establishes a separate legal entity that equally shares responsibility for establishing and operating the entity between physicians and the hospital. Typically, an MSO is not licensed to practice medicine.

Mid-level providers: A subset of licensed nonphysician practitioners that generally practices under the supervision of physicians but is allowed some autonomy in practice, whether in regard to prescriptive authority or the ability to provide some level of independent care.

National Committee on Quality Assurance (NCQA): A nonprofit organization that works to improve the quality of health care through the accreditation of managed care plans.

Network model HMO: An HMO that contracts with many independent physician practices that may also treat other patients who are not enrolled in the plan.

Nonparticipating provider: Providers who have not agreed to accept the Medicare reimbursement amount for every claim. Yet, nonparticipating providers are allowed to accept Medicare assignment on a claim-by-claim basis, if they agree to certain conditions.

Physician-hospital organization (PHO) model: A legal entity formed by a hospital and a group of physicians that combines both parties into a single organization for the purpose of gaining greater negotiating leverage in obtaining managed care contracts.

Physician-hospital organizations: An enterprise that unites a hospital or group of hospitals with a physician organization through a contractual relationship.

Point-of-service (POS) plans: Plans that combine many of the elements of HMOs and PPOs. POS plans are usually an addition to an HMO product that allows members the benefit of seeking care from nonparticipating providers. As with an HMO, when members seek care from in-network providers, they typically pay no deductible or co-insurance. However, similar to a PPO, members are free to seek services outside the network subject to higher cost sharing in the form of deductibles and co-insurance.

Revenue cycle: The process by which a provider practice schedules patients, diagnoses conditions, documents diagnoses, bills payers, and collects billable charges from the payer and the patient to recover revenue for the services provided.

Self-insurance: Self-insuring employers make a conscious choice to undertake the risks associated with the cost of health care and set aside money to pay these costs as they arise. Often, a self-insurer will hire a commercial insurer or third-party administrator to run its medical benefits program and adjudicate claims.

Staff model HMO: An HMO that employs physicians and other providers who treat only the particular HMO's enrollees.

Tangible assets: Physical assets (such as cash, accounts receivable, inventory, property, plant and equipment, and so forth).

Value in place and in use: Premise of value that assumes that the assets will continue to be used as part of an ongoing business enterprise, producing profits as a benefit of ownership.

Vertical integration: The aggregation of dissimilar but related business units, companies, or organizations under a single ownership or management in order to provide a full range of related products and services.

Index

D

E

I

J

K

L

M

N

U

V

W

Printed in the United States
by Baker & Taylor Publisher Services